connected

connected

Christian Parenting in an Age of IM and MySpace

PEGGY KENDALL

Foreword by Leonard Sweet

JUDSON PRESS
PUBLISHERS SINCE 1824
VALLEY FORGE

Judson Press and the author have made every effort to trace the ownership of all quotes. In the event of a question arising from the use of a quote, we regret any error made and will be pleased to make the necessary correction in future printings and editions of this book.

For additional up-to-date resources, helpful tips, and challenging online discussions, visit the author's blog at http://pkendall.squarespace.com/.

Library of Congress Cataloging-in-Publication Data

Kendall, Peggy.
    Connected : Christian parenting in an age of IM and MySpace / Peggy Kendall ; foreword by Leonard Sweet. — 1st ed.
        p. cm.
    ISBN 978-0-8170-1516-9 (pbk. : alk. paper) 1. Parenting—Religious aspects—Christianity. 2. Child rearing—Religious aspects—Christianity. 3. Online social networks. 4. Technology—Religious aspects—Christianity. 5. Internet and teenagers. 6. MySpace (Firm) 7. Instant messaging. 8. Internet—Safety measures. I. Title.
    BV4529.K46 2007
    248.8'45—dc22
                                                                        2007002849

Printed on recycled paper in the U.S.A.

First Edition, 2007.

To my teachers
Nate and Hannah

contents

rewind, fast forward

Irish novelist and playwright John McGahern contends that "There are no days more full in childhood than those days that are not lived at all, the days lost in a book."

When you read that, how do you feel? Do his words make you feel sentimental, nostalgic, even romantic? Now replace that last word, *book*, with *screen* and repeat the sentence. How do you feel after this altered reading?

That difference you feel is the subject of *Connected: Christian Parenting in an Age of IM and MySpace*. Every parent would do well to read this book before we miss the boat, both coming and going, in understanding the cultural shifts that have taken place in our lifetime. The theme of an innocent person trying to figure out a radically different culture is as old as literature, and it has characterized some of the world's greatest literature (e.g., Voltaire's *Candide*). But in our case, that different world is the world of our children, and our children's children.

In Germany this is dubbed the struggle between laptops and lederhosen. I call it the scramble between Google people and Gutenberg people, which forms what Fast Company calls a "population hourglass." At the top of the hourglass are Gutenbergers, who live behind a glass darkly, and that glass is the printed page. At the bottom of the hourglass are Googlers, who are nearly equal in numbers to the Gutenbergers and who also live behind a glass darkly, but that glass is the screen.

The Harry Potter series is the most successful multigenerational book in history for a reason. It comes in two bindings. One for Gutenberg people, many of whom began life when there were no computers, no "boob tubes," no transistors, no birth control pills, no microwave ovens, and no frozen foods. The other binding is for Google people, those aged 17 and under who began life before there were any live web pages, MySpace, YouTube, Second Life, Wii-motes, and Fresh Express.

If we are to build a future that any of us would like to live in, the residents of these different worlds need to learn from one another and talk to each other. Gutenberg people need to sit at the feet of their children and learn to hit the fast forward button; Google people need to sit at the feet of their elders and learn to hit the rewind button, which can reverse and replay the reel of history.

Gutenberg people need to get over their resentment at how existing authorities are undermined by computer technologies. For the first time in history, Googlers do not need authority figures to access information. Googlers are now the experts in important features of how to live and move and have our being in this emerging culture. Gutenbergers have no choice but to learn from their kids how to create a Second Life avatar, play the Wii, and watch videos on our cell phones.

Children have important things to teach adults. If truth be told, they always have. "Unless you become as little children," Jesus warned in Matthew 18:3. We have treated children's spirituality as a stunted, immature version of "adult spirituality" rather than as a fully orbed experience in and of itself. We must come to realize that children have insights into life and navigating the future that we lose at our peril. In fact, the older we get, the worse our eyesight becomes, and the more we need youth to constantly renew our vision.

This will not be easy because, increasingly, postmodern global culture does not like little people. A 2006 United Nations report, put together by a team from UNICEF, ranked Great Britain at the bottom of 21 prosperous nations in its treatment of children. Only 60 percent of British children say their parents talk to them, which means that 40 percent of British children are being raised without the guidance and wisdom of their parents.

While Googlers have a different relationship to knowledge and may not need authority figures to *access* information, they actually need authority figures more than ever: to process and *assess* information. Although the "little-mugs" don't need the "big-jugs" to catch the information that they need, they do need mentors to help them turn this information into knowledge and wisdom, and to help them with the critical skills to assess what is good information versus bad information.

The tale of those of who have traveled this way before must be retold in every generation. This is no exception. Googlers have been raised with little understanding of history or privacy or trust. MySpace has an attitude toward friends that resembles that of Imelda Marcos toward shoes. Blogging can quickly become closed conversations that are full of sound and fury, signifying nothing. Gutenbergers can teach Googlers the wisdom of sometimes needing to feel in our heart what our mind already knows, and other times needing to think in our mind what our heart already knows. Paul warned of those who were "always learning and never able to come to the knowledge of the truth" (2 Timothy 3:7). Googlers collect experiences like Gutenbergers collect things, and the phenomenon of always going to seminars and never doing anything with what is learned there is one of the hallmarks of postmodern culture.

I love this book because it gives practical advice how to build these bridges between Gutenberg people and Google people. Instead of the customary narrative of cultural decline, expressions of cultural anxiety, denunciation of the awfulness of the times, not to mention millennial moanings, what Peggy Kendall gives us are strategies for passing the baton onto succeeding generations without the trade of tirades. Here is an author who is as bothered as I am by why the church isn't galvanized by this new world opening up. Here is an author who says *carpe manana* ("seize tomorrow!").

Pope Benedict XVI celebrated Christmas 2006 at the Vatican with a speech from the central balcony of the face of St. Peter's

Basilica. In this "Urbi et Orbi" ("To the City and To the World") address he admitted that we are living in a postmodern age, an age that needs a Savior like never before. The Pope then urged Christians to "make this message of hope resound in a credible way" in this postmodern culture. This book does precisely that.

Leonard Sweet
Drew Theological School
George Fox University
www.wikiletics.com

introduction

One sunny afternoon as I stood at the window, I heard birds chirping and ducks quacking. I then turned to look at my two teenage children who had just arrived home from school. It was dark in the family study, but through the shadows I could make out my children's faces as the computer screens lit up their glazed and unnatural smiles.

"So how were your days at school?" I cheerily asked. I heard nothing but the sinister clicking of the keyboard keys.

"What did you learn today?" I asked again, hoping for at least a grunt or perfunctory "Nothing." I sat and watched helplessly as my sweet children, who used to be so happy, so engaged, so talkative, typed madly away at their computers, enveloped in a strange and menacing cyber reality.

Being a mom who doesn't take these kinds of things sitting down, I stood up. It was time I did something. I reached for the plug. An unnatural force seemed to be pulling it back, but I took the action I knew needed to be taken. I unplugged the computers.

My children looked up with a start. They blinked. The glazed look in their eyes began to be replaced with real emotion. They smiled and ran to me, embracing me with hugs and kisses.

"Thanks, Mom!" said my seventeen-year-old. "You have saved us from the wicked snare of instant messaging. You have delivered us from the fiendish world of MySpace." With that, my children ran, hand in hand, outside in the sun, and began playing and singing.

I awoke with a start as my own cell-phone–PDA–camera– e-mailing–Web-surfing–texting device vibrated. It was all a dream.

I looked at my handheld—my husband was text-messaging me to say he would be late for dinner. I looked up and realized the computers were still plugged in and my children were still typing messages to their friends. And I was still wondering when life and friendships and growing up had changed so much. There was no doubt about it: my world was full of technology, and my children were using it in ways I had never experienced.

As I sat contemplating what, if anything, I should do, I realized I couldn't just pull the plug. (Actually, I wasn't sure where the plug was anyway.) Not only did my children use the technology in ways I didn't fully understand, but in some odd way, they seemed to be meeting important developmental needs through the technology. And if I were being honest, my children were doing well—they were happy, they had friends, they enjoyed school, they were good at interacting with people, and they had an understanding of who God is and what he expected of them. And if I were being *really* honest, I would have to admit that technology played a big part in helping them do well in each one of those areas.

Scripture exhorts parents to train up children in the way they should go (Proverbs 22:6)—but what does that look like in a culture obsessed with technology, efficiency, and self-satisfaction? How are culture and technology impacting our kids? Is there a "Christian" approach to dealing with teenagers and technology?

Two Extremes

Parents can manage technology in their households in a lot of ways—some ways better than others. One approach is to go cold turkey. This approach has been adopted by a few of my friends who revel in telling me about how they have completely unplugged their homes. Their kids are simply not allowed to go online. One mom told me, "Beth will have to be grown up, living somewhere else, and using her own computer before she's ever allowed to browse the Internet or use Instant Messenger."

That is certainly one approach to handling the problems associated with technology. But I wonder if those unplugged kids are really learning how to operate in today's wired culture. I wonder if they will know how to handle the challenges associated with the online communication that will inevitably become part of their lives. I wonder if they will know how to approach technology, with all its efficiencies, temptations, and relational pitfalls, from a Christian perspective. Certainly unplugging may be appropriate for some families, especially those with young children. However, it may be an extreme approach that doesn't truly help teenagers learn how to deal with something that is a real part of their every-day culture and will certainly become an important part of their adult lives.

On the other hand, I have friends whose kids use instant messaging for hours at a time, spending even more hours creating MySpace profiles and writing on their friends' blogs. When I talk to middle schoolers, they often tell me their parents have no idea what they do online. When I talk with college students, they tell me they wish their parents had placed more limits on what they did in high school. I wonder if by not paying attention to what our kids are doing online, we are relegating them to learn complex and hurtful lessons without our help. I wonder if we are simply tuning out the technology because we feel uncomfortable with it and don't really know what to do.

What is the answer? What do we do with these teens who seem to know so much more about technology than we do and want to use it so very badly? It is my guess that somewhere between the two extremes lies the most productive path. We are the parents. We need to make intentional choices about what our kids do—especially something as significant as how they use technology to enhance their friendships and express themselves. But, because every kid is different and every parent is different, there is no "right" answer as to how we should govern the use of technology.

Opportunity Knocks

It is quite possible that as our teens enter their adolescent years and become more independent, more difficult, and more isolated from us, technology may actually be the thing that reconnects us. We have a lot to learn from our kids, and if we are willing to listen, we may discover remarkable things about our children as they teach us about their technology.

Technology is irrefutably a key part of the lives of many young people. It is the way they connect with friends, participate in community, express themselves, and establish their identity. It is their "lifeline." If that's the case, surely we don't want to react by simply pulling the plug. Instead, we want to better understand how technology has become integrated into their experience. They may just be willing to share part of that experience with us—if only we will ask. This book is designed to help parents figure out how to start the conversation.

Some young people may not be using technology to communicate with their friends. This may be the perfect opportunity for parents to come alongside their children and learn with them how to navigate the benefits and pitfalls of online communication. This book provides information about those benefits and pitfalls.

By figuring out how instant messaging and social networking sites work and how they can be used in positive ways, parents can help their kids make good choices. By understanding some of the ugly aspects of online communication, parents can talk with their kids about what kinds of limits should be established and why. They can also begin a conversation that includes their children's thoughts about technology, friendship, and growing up in this wired world.

Getting Connected

The purpose of this book is to educate, support, and motivate. It came about as a result of questions I have struggled with as I have watched my teenagers spend increasing amounts of time on the computer, using new and confusing technology to meet teenage needs that I met in very different ways when I was their age. I teach at a university full of passionate IMers, bloggers, and online social networkers, and so I began talking to them about what this technology was and how they thought it had impacted them. These discussions turned into formalized studies in which a team of student researchers and I surveyed and interviewed hundreds of college, high school, and middle school students about IM and social networking sites such as MySpace, Facebook, and Xanga. We also interviewed and surveyed parents and youth pastors to get a better perspective on how communication technology is impacting kids at home and at church. Through this research experience I have learned a couple of things.

First, it is clear that online communication is here to stay. Young people have begun to fundamentally change the way they "do" friendships. While certain websites or certain technologies may come and go, the idea of using technology to communicate to friends and to express an emerging identity has been absolutely adopted by a majority of American teenagers.

Second, students *love* their technology. They love using it and they love talking about it. They are utilizing instant messaging and social networking sites to meet developmental needs. Young people find it frustrating when adults talk about these technologies in exclusively negative terms. They consistently ask me to tell parents to "talk to their kids," "ask their kids why they like IM so much," and "ask their kids to show them some of the things they've done with their online profiles." Because communication technology is a significant part of the teenage experience that is often misunderstood, it is wise for us adults to at least contemplate some of the good things technology does for our kids.

Third, IM and social networking sites can be very bad. Not only are they impacting our kids in ways we probably don't realize, but they can breed some very bad social behaviors. I have heard too many stories about bullying, lying, meanness, sexual experimentation, and predatory behavior to think that these technologies are value-neutral. While many of these behaviors are simply an unfortunate part of adolescence, online technology allows students to feel freer to engage in hurtful conduct. As wise parents, we need to come alongside our kids to help them learn how to use these technologies in prudent, thoughtful, and God-honoring ways.

The bottom line is that this topic is of great consequence. Unfortunately, the solution to the questions and challenges associated with teenage use of online communication technology is more complex than simply unplugging the computer. The exciting thing is that God hasn't dumped this mess at our feet to let us sort through on our own. God has promised to provide us with strength, wisdom, and courage as we raise our children. I firmly believe that God can actually work through these technologies to touch teenagers in a way that we might not understand or foresee. Don't forget: God is bigger than the Internet, faster than an instant messenger, and stronger than a MySpace profile. God can use the world's technology to touch uniquely the heart of children who have been raised in a culture decidedly different than the one in which we were raised. As Christian parents, we need to accept the challenge to connect with the lives of our children—even if it means moving beyond the dream world, pulling up to the computer, and signing on.

instant messaging

"Who, Exactly, Is the Messenger, and What Makes Him So Instant?"

B efore we can decide how best to help our teenagers manage the communication technology in their lives, it makes sense to get a clear picture of what the technology is and how kids are using it. Take the case of Sarah, a bright, motivated, sociable eighth grader who loves talking about music, fingernail colors, boys, puppies, and craft projects. Although she has a few friends in her neighborhood, most of her closest friends are either from church or school and live a few miles away. Because she can't drive and her mom works a lot, Sarah often spends time by herself. That is, she did until she got her instant messaging account. Now she is able to hang out with her friends whenever she wants. She does-n't have to pack everything up and walk to a friend's house. She doesn't have to call on the phone and stumble around the house with a receiver glued to her ear. All she has to do is turn on her computer, situate it so she can see the television, find the music files she wants to listen to, position her homework next to the screen, and sign on. She is all set to spend the evening with her friends—without getting behind on her homework, missing her favorite TV show, or bugging her mom and dad.

Sarah is not alone. According to a study done by the Pew Internet and American Life Project released in 2005, two out of every three American teenagers use instant messaging. That means a majority of teenagers across the country pull up to the computer on a regular basis to use technology to help build their friendships. The average teenager begins using IM around sixth grade, and nearly 94 percent of American teenagers use IM by twelfth grade. That's a lot of teenage IMers, which means that instant messaging, in all its many forms, has quietly found its way into the lives of *millions* of teenagers, taking hold of family computers and transforming the way our children do friendships. Because it isn't as flashy as MySpace or as worrisome as violent video games, it doesn't tend to grab our attention. But as we consider the impact technology is having on our kids, we must not overlook this fundamental form of online teenage communication.

Learning about instant messaging is useful because it is intricately woven into most other online communication tools. For instance, when kids use MySpace to post things for everyone to see, they usually use IM to talk about what it all means. When kids play online video games, they often use IM or chat functions to talk about what else is going on in their worlds. When kids walk around with their cell phones at their fingertips, they are often text-messaging each other, using the same technology as that found in instant messaging. Utilizing real-time online text conversations to connect with one another is an essential part of how today's young people have integrated technology into their lives.

Another reason to increase our understanding of IM is that it points to the fundamental way teens have shifted how they communicate. While MySpace certainly dominates media headlines with stories of predators and pornography, IM may have a more far-reaching impact on our young people. Today's teenagers are learning how to build friendships, participate in community, and see themselves in relation to others and to God all through a computer. Many kids actually prefer to communicate with each other by typing things into a computer, thereby reducing relationships and rich conversations into pages of text. That's significant. That's why it makes sense to begin a conversation about teenage use of communication technology with an examination of this fairly tame-looking but highly influential tool. The first step in helping kids learn to use this quiet but powerful form of communication wisely is to better understand the "what" and the "how" of IM.

The "What" of Instant Messaging

Instant messaging is a technology that has been around since the late 1970s when engineers and other sophisticated computer users began talking in real time using their UNIX/LINUX systems. For many of us, the late seventies were more about bell-bottoms, Donny Osmond, and Pong than giant, room-sized computers. However, these computer pioneers were able to communicate with each other around the globe as one letter popped up at a time. While not the zippiest form of communication, these users set the stage for a communication system that would eventually move well beyond the small, well-controlled and highly complex computer network designed for academics and military personnel. It wasn't long before the technology became more user-friendly, providing the foundation for real-time interaction applications like chat rooms and MUDs (multi-user domains), where users gather to play games. But it wasn't until 1996 that the true precursor to today's IM system was introduced. ICQ (an IM-style play on the words "I seek you") was the first online communication system to offer a "presence information feature" whereby users were able to see who else in the network was online and available. In 2002 America Online (AOL), a division of Time Warner, patented Instant Messenger, and the rest is virtual history.[1]

In case you still aren't sure what exactly instant messaging is, let's look at America Online's definition: their Instant Messenger is "a free online service that lets you communicate with family, friends, and coworkers in real time. Using a buddy list feature, you can see when your buddies are online and available to instant message."[2] That means kids can type to each other in real time, participating in exchanges that resemble real-life conversations but without all the extra nonverbal and contextual information. The

3

most popular instant messaging services currently include MSN Messenger, AOL Instant Messenger, Yahoo! Messenger, Skype, Google Talk, .NET Messenger Service, Jabber, QQ, iChat, and ICQ.[3] As long as two users are in the same system, they can download IM for free and begin sending real-time, personal messages to one another. Users also have the choice of entering an IM chat room with their friends where everyone in the room can see what each chatter is saying.

E-mail's Speedy Cousin

Those are the instant messaging basics. But that's not where the story ends. Some of the additional features of IM mean more fun and greater impact on teenage culture and relationships. We can draw a parallel with e-mail, a technology tool that many adults have begun integrating into daily life (a tool, which, by the way, has been labeled by many teenagers as a tool left over for "adults" who haven't figured out how to use anything better). E-mail has been around for a number of years and slowly but surely has become an accepted, even expected, part of the workplace landscape.

If you use e-mail on a regular basis, you know how it truly can help you communicate with others in a convenient and nonintrusive way. One of the drawbacks, however, is that e-mail has made us virtually accessible all hours of the day, creating a tyranny of the immediate. You may have felt it—a certain nagging quality about unanswered e-mails, each calling in insidious ways for you to drop the things you already planned and labeled important, the things happening in the here and now, to respond to the electronic page of text sent by someone sitting in a room far away. E-mail technology has not only accelerated the rate at which we communicate with people, but it has also dramatically increased the perceived speed at which we are expected to respond.

In many ways, e-mail is instant messaging's slower cousin. Just like e-mail, IM is a conversation in a text box. It has become an expected and integrated part of adolescent culture. It has changed users' sense of timeliness by making them feel they may miss something important if they leave the technology unattended. That, however, is where the similarities end.

Unlike e-mail, instant messaging operates in *real* time. This ability to send and receive messages instantaneously has a number of interesting consequences. First, it makes interactions more about conversation and less about simply sending messages. Shared meaning and two-way understanding is still a problem but is much more important in an IM context than in an e-mail situation.

Second, real-time communication creates a false sense of reality as it mimics aspects of face-to-face conversations. With IM it is easy to imagine two people sitting around a table having a great conversation. As will be discussed further in chapter 4, the conversational environment created by the technology makes it much easier to blur the distinction between real and virtual.

Third, IM creates an uncanny quality of shared social presence. Even though the two users may be in very different places, they are truly "spending time" together. The "buddy" feature allows friends to "share space" and hang out with each other by letting everyone within a group of friends know when each person is signed on. Even when two friends aren't talking to each other, they are still connected, much as if they are hanging out at someone's house. And think about it: when we talk about "hanging out with friends," that often means just being together—not necessarily talking together—just sharing time and space. As a result, teens can be signed on and hanging out with their friends while they accomplish other tasks—the same way a group of friends might study or watch TV together—no talking, just hanging. As pointed out by Michelle, a seventh grader who loves to IM with her friends, "My mom freaks out because she thinks I'm IMing the whole time I'm on the computer. A lot of the time, I'm just doing homework or listening to music with my friends." Clearly, the real-time aspect of IM has fundamentally changed what it means to "spend time together" and "hang out with friends."

The "How" of Instant Messaging

Getting Connected

The sign-on. Because instant messaging has become primarily a teenage "hang-out" tool, a number of uniquely teenage IM

5

conventions have developed. If we want to better understand how our kids use and need the technology, it makes sense to understand some of these quirky "teenage" IM characteristics. The first has to do with the sign-on. While each teenage IMer must have a sign-on name, many have more than one. The reasoning behind multiple names is quite strategic. When teens go online, they may or may not want to talk with everyone on their buddy list. Maybe they are mad at a group of friends, maybe a friend is getting on their nerves, maybe they are tired and don't have the energy to manage a lot of conversations, maybe they don't want Mom and Dad to see particular buddies, or maybe they kind of "like" one of the buddies on the list but aren't quite ready to "make the move." By choosing which sign-on name they use, they are choosing which buddy list will appear and which group of friends will see that they are ready to chat.

While some IM programs have become increasingly adept at allowing users to pick and choose which buddies will see them "online and available" and which ones will see them as "busy," many teens find that by using different screen names, they can more easily manage the various parts of their lives. For instance, Maria might have a particular screen name she gives to her friends from camp and another more confidential screen name given only to close friends. She may have certain friends "blocked" under those screen names, while she gives another name to everyone she can think of. Finally, she may have a screen name kept primarily for deceptive purposes, allowing Maria to pretend to be someone she is not. By choosing which screen name to sign on with, Maria (and other users like her) is choosing which group of friends she wants to "hang out" with.

MAKE A CONNECTION: **Next time you are on the IM log-in page, notice the screen names. If your child has more than one, a terrific opportunity might exist to begin a conversation about how those different screen names are used. You may find that your teen has developed a sophisticated strategy of managing the many disparate parts of a complex social life.**

"Online and available." Once users sign on to IM, they can choose whether the people on their buddy list will see them as "online and available" or "offline" or "busy." Keeping track of each IMer's "online status" is something every user on a particular computer should be aware of. Sometimes the IM program starts as soon as the computer is turned on, regardless of who is using the computer. That means you may get on the family computer and everyone on your teen's buddy list suddenly sees "online and available" next to your teen's IM name. They, of course, would assume it is your teen who is online and available—not an unaware parent who has just sat down to catch up on the news.

You may find yourself cruising along on the computer and suddenly one of your teen's buddies pops in with a "Hey, how's it going?" As tempting as it may be to pretend to be your teen and ask questions like "So what do you really think about my mom?" you may want to reconsider. I try to fight the urge and instead like to see my daughter's friends squirm as I let them know "Mom" has just signed on. Once kids find out they are talking with a parent, they either suddenly become polite, saying things like "Oh. Hello, Mrs. Kendall" or sign off more quickly than you can say instant message. One parent says she regularly takes these opportunities to talk to her teenager's friends. She says it's a great way to get caught up on their lives. The drawback is that her daughter becomes completely mortified when she finds out her mom has been on IM again. However you deal with the sign-on function, it is important to pay attention to whether the IM program is running and who may be assuming the IMer is currently logged on.

PARENT TIP: **To make sure the instant messaging program doesn't automatically start as soon as someone signs on, simply go to the IM default settings and change how and when the program begins.**

Buddy Lists

One final element of getting connected has to do with whom your teen is talking to. Remember back in high school when you could tell who the popular kids were? They always had more friends hanging out by their locker, they had more dates, and on special occasions, they got more flowers or cards than anyone else. Now, let's face it—not all those kids who hung out with the popular students were that great of friends with them (or at least that's what I kept telling myself). But just by virtue of there being lots of friends in the vicinity, they were labeled "popular."

The same is true for "buddy lists." Most programs will allow a maximum of two hundred buddies, and lots of teenage IMers have filled their buddy lists to the max. Now don't confuse an IM "buddy" with a real-life buddy—you know, the kind of "buddy" we had growing up, the kind with whom we would laugh, go to the mall, and stick by through thick and thin. Nope. This kind of "buddy" is usually one who takes up space in the buddy list. That's it. Once someone is accepted by your teen as a buddy, his or her name will show up on the side of the IM screen. For many buddies, that's where the "budship" ends.

Actually, the whole IM buddy thing is pretty interesting. Just like "friends" on MySpace, the more buddies someone has, the more popular he or she is perceived to be. As a result, students are always on the lookout for new buddies. Buddy names are enthusiastically shared between friends and friends of friends. For instance, when teens meet for the first time in a face-to-face situation, it's natural for them to share their IM screen names. Not only do they get a new name to put on their buddy list, but they also are able to get to know that new person in an environment that is much less awkward and forced. I always have to chuckle when kids can't actually remember the name of the person they met on a church retreat or at a school function, but they know their IM name and have been talking with them for weeks.

While making new friends by openly sharing screen names can be a positive thing, doggedly pursuing long buddy lists can result in some pretty negative situations. Many kids with long buddy lists simply don't have a clue who some of the people are who appear on their list—either they never knew or they knew and forgot. That means they may be interacting with strangers. Now, certainly not all strangers are bad. Kids can make some very good friends through IM. However, when teens interact with people they have never met in a face-to-face context, there is much greater room for deception. There are bad people out there looking for ways to build relationships with naïve young IMers. As we will discuss in later chapters, instant messaging can be a pathway that leads straight to a teenager's heart, and predators know it. Therefore, teens who IM strangers—even though they seem nice and claim to be a friend of a friend—are opening themselves up to a dangerous side of online communication.

That having been said, it's not quite time to run and grab your teen's keyboard from his or her fingertips. According to almost every IMer we have talked with and surveyed, teenagers tend to use instant messaging to enhance their existing face-to-face relationships. When it comes down to it, most teens see the potential dangers of IMing people they don't know, especially when they have wary parents who tenaciously remind them of what it means to have a true buddy.

MAKE A CONNECTION: **A buddy list can serve as an alert to parents who are concerned about some of the more troubling aspects of online communication technology. Challenge your teen to identify every person on his or her buddy list. This will be especially fun if the list is long. If your teen doesn't know who someone is, can't remember who he or she is, or has never met the buddy, ask that the name be removed.**

All in all, a buddy list can say quite a bit about a teen. In many ways, it says who he or she is hanging out with. And just as a parent will naturally ask about the friends with whom a teenager is going to go to a movie or a party, having a chat about a buddy list can be one way to keep communication open about teenage friendships and social networks. The best thing is that teens usually don't mind talking about their buddies. In fact, many teenage IMers recommend that parents get involved in their child's IM life by talking about buddies. For many, talking about *who* they are talking to is much less invasive and more palatable than parents wanting to know *what* they are talking about.

9

IMspeak

While *who* teens talk to is important, *how* they talk can be just as intriguing. If you have an IMer at home, you can probably resonate with my experience. A few years ago it became obvious that my son was not terribly forthcoming about his computer time—at least he wasn't giving me as much information as I thought should be shared between a loving mother and her almost grown-up son. I knew I needed a new strategy to get that information. I decided to get sneaky (tell me you haven't done the same thing). One evening as my son was intently typing away in multiple IM conversations, I nonchalantly glanced over his shoulder as I walked by. I almost saw something before he quickly pulled his chair around, blocking my view. Not prone to giving up that easily, I walked by again. This time I was in "stealth" mode, making no audible sound as I slowly passed by. I read something, but I must admit, I was perplexed. I could see the conversation, yet I had no idea what it meant. Now, I know a little French and can identify Pig Latin, but this IMspeak was new to me.

If you have read any teenage IM conversations, you know there exists a very distinctive online language. While some of the necessity for a specialized language probably arose from attempts by mothers like me trying to read over their teenagers' shoulders, much of it has arisen out of a need for teens to type faster while including enough information to communicate effectively.

To clarify meaning. It is no surprise that one of the things IMers complain about most is misunderstandings that arise from people misinterpreting what they type. One of the biggest problem areas has to do with sarcasm. Think about it: sarcasm is saying the exact opposite of what you mean. The way someone knows when you are being sarcastic is by the way you change your voice or your facial expressions. Try this little experiment: Say, "Yeah, I hate that stuff" two times—once as if you really hate it and the second as if you are joking. By using your voice and facial expressions, you were able to communicate two very different messages. Unfortunately, both meanings are typed the same way.

The solution? Add some extra information: "omg, i hate that stuff :-) jk." By adding a little information, IMers can make sure their friends better understand their intent. Acronyms such as **omg** (oh, my gosh), **jk** (just kidding), **tbh** (to be honest), and **imho** (in my humble opinion) add the necessary context for a comment. Emoticons like :-) (smiley face), B-) (cool dude), :"> (blushing face), ;-) (winky face), or >-((mad face) add emotional cues necessary to better interpret what a fellow IMer means. Clearly, teenage IMers have adapted language and special keyboard strokes to more effectively communicate in a text-based medium.

To type faster. Another limitation of the IM medium relates to the time-intensive nature of typing everything out. While most teenagers have become speedy typists, the process of typing out a complex emotional message may take way too much time. IM-speak helps teens better communicate complex ideas in a short amount of time. It also streamlines the process. For instance, capital letters and correct punctuation, while a big deal to English teachers and worried parents, is not a big deal to IMers. Forget them. In fact, you can forget many of the extra vowels that just tend to slow things down; for instance, "hw r u i m fn" is quick, easy, and to the point. IMspeak also includes acronyms that can communicate complex thoughts with just a few strokes. Try these:

ATM. No, not a cash machine: "at the moment."

CUL8R. In true license plate fashion: "See you later."

TTFN. Any good Winnie the Pooh parent should know this one: "Ta-ta for now."

K. Yeah, this one is a big time saver: "OK."

LOL. This one is pretty old school—every parent should know it: "laugh out loud."

POS. Watch out for this one: "parent over shoulder."

SD4YM. The creator of this one definitely has hip hop stardom in his or her future: "Save the drama for yo mama."

LSHIPAL. This one is my all-time favorite: "laughed so hard I peed a little."[4]

To communicate culture. IMspeak clearly helps to combat some of the limitations of a text-based, keyboard-based medium. Teens have taken a stark, dull form of communicating and turned it into something that is fun and efficient at the same time. But

11

IMspeak does more than just meet the demands of the medium. It also signifies the interaction as foundationally adolescent. Just as you can always pick out the youth room in a church or the youth magazines in a bookstore, IMspeak is a way that young people establish their identity and communicate elements about their culture. It's one of the unique functions of language—it says something about those who use it.

And before you throw up your hands in despair of kids who just don't know how to use English, keep in mind that specialized language and jargon is not limited to the youth culture. Think about it: doctors use it, teachers use it, even Christians use it. We all use jargon that communicates something about who we are, what we value, and how we think. Jargon helps us condense ideas that everyone in the group already understands. It makes communicating more efficient. The problem arises when someone from outside the group tries to understand what the jargon means. You experience this when you go to a doctor's office and feel foolish because you don't understand what he or she is saying. You see the doctor's mouth moving, and you recognize the words as English, but you just don't quite grasp the full meaning of the message. You see it when someone who has not been raised in a church comes to a worship service and gets a dazed look on his face when someone tells him about "sin," "salvation," and "grace." Everyone else seems to understand it, but the "outsider" isn't privy to the broad implications and deep meanings of the unfamiliar concepts. Jargon has a way of bonding groups together while separating those who are in the group from those who are not.

Jargon can also give us a glimpse into the values of a culture. In the case of IMspeak, it would seem that those who use it value efficiency, fun, and a bit of "bucking the system." Deep thoughts are articulated with just a few letters, making IMing quick, easy, fun, and maybe a little simplistic. Grammar rules are replaced with rules that highlight fun and group secrets. Take, for example, the common practice of developing a "code" to alert buddies that a parent has entered the room. Teens say they often have more fun coming up with the code than actually using it to deceive their parents. I'm not sure I believe that one! But whatever the case, IMspeak is a uniquely teenage language. If we keep our eyes and minds open, we may be better able to understand some of the things our kids value and enjoy.

Keeping that in mind, it is important that we adults seek to have both patience and a certain degree of respect for IMspeak. To be honest, it drives me crazy that my kids are using such bad grammar and spelling. I have nightmares that they will forget everything they learned in English class all these years! All those spelling tests we studied for—ugh! But, IMspeak is the way they communicate on IM. It makes good use of the medium, and it communicates important things about their culture.

MAKE A CONNECTION: **Ask your teen to teach you some of the abbreviations he or she uses on IM. Try typing an instant message and have your teen show you how to type it faster using IMspeak, or have your teen type a message to you using IMspeak to see if you can figure it out. Be aware: some teens may not want their parents knowing and using teenage language, so be sensitive to how willing your child might be IMing you using this very private communication.**

The "Art" of Instant Messaging

Self-Expression

When I ask middle schoolers what they like best about IM, they consistently say, "It's fun!" Honestly, I don't see sitting at a computer, typing my heart out as being particularly "fun"—it seems a lot more like work than a good time. I, however, have not mastered the *art* of IM.

As can be seen with the appeal of social networking sites like MySpace, young people love to be creative and express unique aspects of their personalities in a fun and dynamic way. Online IM providers such as AIM and MSN Messenger have become quite good at offering teenagers opportunities to express themselves. For instance, in many IM programs, a user is able to use a photo or create an avatar (a stylized cartoon figure that can be customized to look like the user) that will pop up next to the teen's name on other users' buddy lists. Photos are often changed according to the user's mood or recent interests, and some avatars have faces that will change according to the emoticons being used. IMers can also customize their "IMvironments," or "interactive backgrounds" that pop up with the IM screen. The top five Yahoo! Messenger IMvironments for the week I last looked included Harry Potter, New York, Maybelline, soccer, and NASCAR themes. Creative backgrounds can help an IM user design an IMvironment that communicates a little something about who he or she is.

Another way teenagers personalize their IM experience is to create fun "away messages." An away message is something that pops up when the person is signed on but is not able to talk—much like a voice mail greeting. Teens get very creative with these messages, posting poems, homework questions, invitations, jokes, blog links, or annoying noises for people who are looking for a chat. Away messages can keep the IM connection going even when the IMer has taken a virtual break.

Teens can also have fun within their actual conversations. Most IM programs have a host of emoticons users can use to "spice up" their conversations. Some emoticons include the usual smiley and winky faces, while others have fully animated faces to act out a laugh, a wink, or a grimace. Nudges or freezes that make a buddy's screen move can add emphasis to a particularly important comment, while a variety of fonts, colors, and sounds can add flare to otherwise dry exchanges of text. Users can also share music files, pictures, and web links over IM and listen to the same song as they laugh at the same pictures and browse the same websites. By the time this paragraph reaches your hands, there may be dozens more fun things for IMers to do that I can't even imagine at this point. The bottom line? Instant messaging can be fun—really.

MAKE A CONNECTION: Ask your IMer to show you some of the "fun" things about IM. Take a look at the photo or picture that pops up when your teen signs on—ask her why he or she chose it.

Multitasking

IMspeak is certainly an important distinctive of teenage instant messaging, as are the creative ways teens embellish their conversation. Another notable distinctive has to do with how young people actually use IM. If you have teenage IMers at home, you've seen it. In fact, you may have sat back, your jaw hanging open, watching your child accomplish multitasking feats of which you have never dreamed. IMing is designed to be a conversation between two users. But when you have two hundred buddies, how on earth could you limit yourself to talking to only one person at a time? No problem for accomplished IMers. Most of the teens I interviewed said they usually have three to five conversations going at the same time—and that's on a slow night. When things get really poppin', they can manage as many as ten or fifteen at once (although they did admit that fifteen was pushing it).

Keep in mind that these are real conversations. They are also different conversations—each one probably covering very different topics, each with its own mood and flow. Sometimes a conversation whips by as fast as a teen can type (and believe me—that's fast!), while at other times conversations will start and stop, intertwined with homework, supper, soccer, and TV shows. Each time a friend signs on, the computer bleeps. Each time a friend writes something, a new screen pops up. Each time a friend signs off, a door closes. (I won't even tell you about how freaked out I used to get when I kept hearing doors slam late at night. My kids finally told me it was coming from the computer and not some creepy stalker. After that I had a little "talk" with my instant messaging man.) Well, with all the bleeps, dings, screens, door slams, and frenetic typing, it is truly an amazing sight to watch an experienced IMer during the course of a good IM night. Keep in mind, all of this happens at the same time they say they are working on their homework!

Teenage IMers are multitaskers. The way they use the technology has helped them develop a whole set of skills that most adults don't understand, don't value, and don't have. Now, I always thought I was the quintessential multitasker. After all, I'm a mother—isn't that what mothers do? How many times have I gotten dinner ready, watched the evening news, fed the dog, helped the kids with their homework, and listened to my husband's hard day at work—all at the same time? Well, my multitasking skills are nothing compared to what my kids have.

Take, for example, my multitasking meltdown. I had been IMing for about six months. I'll admit, it was pretty hard at first since no one would be my IM buddy. Okay, I still don't have any buddies, but I have learned to IM my kids. One day as I was typing to my daughter (who was in the next room), my husband signed on from work and started a conversation. All of a sudden, I was confronted with two separate conversations. Just when I finished one thought with my daughter, my husband would pop up with a comment. I went back and forth for about two minutes until I put down the computer and ran out of the room yelling, "Help! My brain is about to explode!" True to form, my daughter sent me an instant message to find out what the problem was. This, of course, was at the same time she was playing Wheel of Fortune with a friend in South Carolina, sharing jokes with a friend from school, counseling a friend who lived down the road, and finishing up her math.

Kids can do a lot of things at the same time. But that doesn't mean they do each thing well. Unfortunately, very few studies have been done to examine the cognitive impact IM is having on our children. I will further address the relational impact of multitasking in upcoming chapters, but note here that doing too many things at once may result in lower-quality outcomes for each task. In other words, multitasking may result in less concentration on homework, less focus on establishing shared meaning with a friend, and less thought about what should be said and what shouldn't be said in a complex virtual social environment.

MAKE A CONNECTION: **Have your IMer explain to you some of the limits he has set on multitasking. For instance, how many conversations are too many? At what point does he decide to end conversations to concentrate on other things? What kind of homework is okay to IM with and what kind is not so good?**

Clearly, instant messaging is a uniquely teenage technology that has allowed young people to create their own space. Young people like it because it is fun, it provides a unique way to express themselves, and it is an easy way to manage the many different parts of their high-tech lives. By better understanding why teens like IM so much and how they use it, we can be better situated to help them manage the role technology plays in their relationships. Things have clearly changed since we were teenagers. Much like the sand lot of the 1950s, the burger joint of the '60s, and the mall of the '80s, instant messaging is a technology tool that provides a way for teens in a postmodern era to hang out with their friends. Our kids have learned to meet key social and developmental needs in a wired world. If you have kids who IM, I lay a challenge at your feet. Try IMing. Have your teens help you set up an account. Find a buddy or two—or force your children to be your buddies! Once you get going, you will begin to have a much better understanding of the strengths and limitations of this truly significant form of communication.

Instant Messaging Discussion Starters

Uses. Ask your teen what he or she does on IM. What is his or her favorite thing about it?

Screen names. Find out if your teen has more than one.

Buddy lists. Make sure your teen knows every one of his or her buddies personally.

IMspeak. Try to learn the language—it's addictive!

IM creativity. Ask your teen about the fun things on IM.

Multitasking. Talk with your teen about the limitations of multitasking—and the benefits.

17

social networking

"If MySpace Is Their Space, Is Their Space like My Space?"

What is the first thing you think of when someone mentions MySpace? Before I started looking into the technology, the picture that would flood my mind would be that of some creepy-looking overweight, middle-aged man who hadn't shaved in weeks, sitting in front of a computer in a dimly lit, run-down studio apartment. As "after-school time" rolled around, he would feed his only friend, a mangy, flea-infested dog, and log onto MySpace. His MySpace profile proudly displayed a picture of a seventeen-year-old, buff-looking guy that he found on some webpage. He would bounce from webpage to webpage, telling girls how pretty they were, asking them to meet him in a dark alley. In my mind, this fictional man represented MySpace. And every time I turned on the news and heard about some other innocent girl being stalked or lured into a life of pain and misery through MySpace, that picture was only sharpened and intensified.

At one point about two years ago, however, I began to experience a loud sense of dissonance. At the same time I viewed MySpace and other social networking sites as dens of sin, pornography, and predators, I also heard my college students talk about how much fun they had on Facebook (college students' equivalent of MySpace). Keep in mind, these were good students. They were bright, honest, kind, and just plain good Christian young people. And they loved their social networking sites. The dissonance soon became loud enough for me to find out what social networking was all about.

After many class discussions, hallway conversations, and interrogations over coffee, I have learned a few things from my students. First, students use MySpace and other social networking sites—a lot. They put things on their sites, they read their friends' sites, they find out what is happening and what is so *not* happening, they find out who is dating whom and who is mad at whom, and they express some of their very deepest feelings and convictions. Quite honestly, that makes spaces like MySpace a pretty important kind of online technology.

The other thing I have learned is that social networking sites, most specifically MySpace, are full of both wonderful potential and imminent danger. As I have visited student sites, I have seen some beautiful things. The way that some of my students talk about what it means to be a follower of Christ and how that changes every area of their life is awe-inspiring. I have also seen profiles that made me very sad. Some profiles are full of raw emotion, vulgar language, violence, and pornography. Some communicate something very different about teenagers than what I might see at church or school.

I guess the thing I am most moved to share is that social networking sites can take on a significant role in the lives of teenagers as they figure out how to connect in a world that is so very different from the world in which we were raised. At the same time, sites such as MySpace are full of bad things. Naïve, vulnerable, or confused teenagers can find plenty of ways to get into trouble on MySpace. Unfortunately for those of us who like things in nice, neat boxes, MySpace can be both very good and very bad. So where does that leave parents? Where does this leave Christian parents who want to protect children at the same time we want to teach them how to be bright lights for Christ in a world that so desperately needs him? It leaves us with a very clear challenge: we need to know what our kids are doing. We need to come alongside our kids and help them navigate their technology in a very confusing world.

MySpace History

A working knowledge of the technology is the first step in figuring out how to help our kids manage this very complex and significant technology. Let's start with the history. As I write, MySpace is the leader in social networking sites. In a watershed moment in midsummer 2006, MySpace was named by Hitwise, an organization that monitors Internet use, as "the most popular site on the Web," beating out Google, Yahoo!, and eBay.[1] That means more people access MySpace than any other site on the Internet. On a typical day, MySpace adds about 230,000 users—roughly the population of Scottsdale, Arizona.[2] To say that MySpace is big is an understatement, as every day millions of people access MySpace to get caught up on the lives of their friends.

Surprisingly, for being as big as it is, MySpace was not online until 2003. Can you imagine? MySpace, one of the biggest things to hit this country, utterly transforming the Gen-Me culture, has been around for only a few years! Clearly, the creators of MySpace hit a market need when they started out. I doubt they realized how badly people wanted to find connections in this culture and how that would translate into explosive growth for a fairly simple piece of Internet technology.

Tom Anderson and Chris DeWolfe began working together to lay the MySpace foundations in early 2000. Anderson saw potential with things like dating services and online communities like BlackPlanet and AsianAvenue, but he felt that these sites were "thinking way too small."[3] The thought was that the ungoverned, personally liberating space found on the Internet was well positioned to help people connect with each other. Anderson and DeWolfe were especially interested in how the Internet could be used to free the music industry from the restraints placed on it by big recording labels. They had a passion for helping new bands connect with audiences that would support and encourage their music.

Obviously, something about the free and open space appealed to music lovers and Internet users alike. While MySpace has certainly changed since its inception, you can still find the heavy influence of music and free expression ingrained in the format. If a singer wants to be heard, he or she is on MySpace—regardless of popularity. If a band is looking for new fans, they have a MySpace profile with lots of music clips for users to download and share. There is something about the antiestablishment feel of MySpace, however, that has an especially broad appeal for Internet users. From the beginning, other social networking sites such as friendster.com had lots of rules and guidelines for users to abide by. MySpace users find freedom to express themselves without fear of being kicked off.

As wildly popular as MySpace is, it shouldn't be surprising that corporate America has taken notice. After all, in a place like MySpace, millions of young adult users are just sitting there waiting to be persuaded to buy something. The best part is that these users represent one of the most desirable and profitable market segments in the country. Try as they might to keep MySpace free from corporate influence, Anderson and DeWolfe sold MySpace to Rupert Murdoch's News Corp for $580 million dollars in 2005. By all indications it was a steal. While the numbers are not publicly known, it is estimated that one month of advertising on MySpace brings in as much as $40 million in ad revenue, accounting for nearly 10 percent of all Internet display ad impressions in the United States.[4]

And there are plenty of plans to capitalize on the success of the MySpace brand. The development of MySpace fashion, the merging of MySpace and other News Corp holdings including Fox News, the expansion of partnerships with eBay and Amazon, and even the advancement of MySpace branding and promotion of young adult television shows, music, and various consumer products are just a few of the things in the works. One of the significant challenges of branding MySpace, however, has to do with the increasingly negative perception people have toward MySpace. With every state attorney general or victimized teen who brings MySpace into court, one more negative message is associated with the MySpace brand. It is possible that where politicians and law enforcement officials have failed to bring MySpace into line, market forces and a desire to make a dollar will ultimately serve to rein in the free-wheeling free expression of the wide-open space known as MySpace.[5]

MAKE A CONNECTION: **If your child uses MySpace, ask if he or she sees the influence of music in the site. Also ask your teen about the "bucking the system" attitude MySpace started out with–does it still exist? What does your teen think about it?**

The New Locker Hangout

So, that's where MySpace came from. How and why this idea for promoting bands has captivated an entire generation of young people is something of a mystery. One thing is certain, however: MySpace is somehow meeting some deep-felt needs that our kids have. And keep in mind that these needs, for the most part, are the same needs we had when we were their age—we just went about meeting those developmental social needs in less technological ways.

For just a moment, think back with me to a place you may have tried hard to forget: junior high. Try to remember past the acne problems, the agonizing clothing decisions, and the true emotional and physical pain associated with talking to the opposite sex. Think about where you hung out with your friends.

At Fred Moore Junior High, it was the second-floor lockers before school. As the buses dropped us off, we would congregate around the lockers. We would unpack our book bags at the same time we got caught up on all the social news. We would find out who liked whom and who was fighting. We would share makeup tips. We would complain about our parents. We would tell jokes, listen to music, and laugh about things that happened at a weekend party. Every now and then a cute boy would walk by and we would all shudder and dream about dating. Often friends would introduce other friends as they stopped by on their way to class. There were a lot of different groups that

23

hung out at the lockers, and we had an understanding of who it was okay to talk with and who was a little too cool, uncool, or even a little too dangerous to stand next to. The second-floor lockers created a public meeting space where we were able to hang out with friends and grow in our understanding of what it meant to be part of a social group.

Now, I don't know where your social hangout was, but my guess is that sometimes things got a bit dicey. Some of the kids swore, some of them caught a smoke in the bathroom before going to their lockers, sometimes there were fights, and sometimes couples would go back in the corner and make out. It was a very good thing there were adults in the vicinity to make sure things didn't get too out of control. By definition, hanging out as a teenager means you learn how to act outside of the direct control of adults. It means you make some bad choices. It also means you make some very good choices, meet some very nice people, learn some very important things about yourself, and create some very good memories.

In many ways, MySpace has become the new teenage hangout. By keeping in mind your teenage hangout as well as some of the functions it played in helping you develop into a mature adult, you can get a better understanding of what your kids are doing online and why they think it is so doggone cool.

Finding the Space: The Art of Choosing a Site

At Fred Moore Junior High, different groups hung out at different places. I never ventured upstairs to the third-floor lockers because those kids were older and not much fun. I also stayed away from the basement, because that's where the rough kids hung out who worked on cars and, I was pretty sure, did drugs. Where I hung out depended a lot on where my friends were. While I could choose to hang out in a place that was cleaner or quieter or less stinky, I was pretty much relegated to spending time in the same space as my friends.

The same is true for social networking sites such as MySpace. Although MySpace is currently the biggest (and probably the baddest) social networking site on the block, there are a lot of other sites young people go to connect with one another. For instance, facebook.com is currently the second largest social networking site and ranks as the seventh most frequented site on the Internet.[6] It tends to be preferred by college students and, until recently, was restricted to users who had an edu e-mail address; in other words, students who were affiliated with a college. This perception of restricted access seems to make many college students feel that Facebook is safer than MySpace. Because users can limit access of their sites to people who are from their school, it has a more intimate, controlled feeling. It also lacks many of the tools found on MySpace that allow users to customize their profiles, meaning that the environment in Facebook is more uniform, lacking that out-of-control feeling often found on MySpace.

However, while Facebook *feels* more controlled, there is evidence to suggest that unwelcome guests can feel just as at home in Facebook as in MySpace. For instance, it has become a common practice for employers to do background checks on potential employees—checking both MySpace and Facebook for information that may give new insight into the after-hours behavior of young people who are hoping to become part of their organizations. Schools have begun using Facebook to monitor student use of alcohol and drugs. Just a few weeks ago, one of my college students was horrified to learn that her high school sister had just opened a Facebook account and was routinely reading all about her friends, her weekends, and her new and exciting love life. I think the thing that really undid my student was the fact that her parents routinely monitored her sister's use of the computer. Let's just say, my student had a bit of a Facebook "awakening." In summary, Facebook is a social networking site that focuses on a slightly different market than MySpace. It seems to be a bit tamer but is certainly open to the same kinds of misuse and dangers as those found on any other social networking site.

In addition to MySpace and Facebook, a number of other, smaller sites invite users to connect with new friends. For instance, friendster.com is referred to as the "grandparent" of the social networking craze because it has been around longer than most other sites designed for the general Internet population. Xanga, the third largest social networking site, and Livejournal were also around before MySpace but cater more to those who want to blog and journal. Yahoo! 360 is a newer site with some interesting twists worth keeping an eye on.[7] Other sites have found their niche with specific audiences. For instance, the mom network (www.clubmom.com) is a place for older networkers, Library Thing is for those who like to read, LinkedIn is for those focused on making business connections, Black Planet focuses on issues related to African Americans, and Vampire Freaks is designed especially for the Goth community.

A number of small Christian networking sites also exist, including christianster.com and holypal.com. Their creators are trying to find a way to let students experience the joys of social networking in a space that is much more positive and controlled. It is unclear how many teenagers actually use these sites, but in many ways, what parents deem as the strength of Christian social networking sites may ultimately be seen as a weakness by the very young people who choose whether to log on. As students search for places to hang out with their friends, the natural tendency is to try and find a place that is out of the direct control of parents and other adults. And when it gets right down to it, as good as these sites look and as beneficial as they may be, individual students often have very little to say about where their group of friends will locate. After all, it is hard to have a blast networking with your friends when all your friends use a different site.

MAKE A CONNECTION: **If your child doesn't use MySpace but has been systematically lobbying you for permission for access, try looking at some of the alternative sites. Visit the sites together, and if you decide it looks like a good first step, ask your child to persuade a few friends to try out the alternative site as well. Keep checking back with your child to find out if the site is what you both had hoped for.**

Social networking sites each have their own characteristics. Each one draws a different type of user or social group. Unfortunately, the most popular site, the one where most kids hang out, is also the least monitored, and possibly, because of its wide use, is the most dangerous and destructive site of all.

Profiling the Space: The Art of Managing an Impression

Once a teenager figures out where his or her friends are hanging out, the next step is to craft the image. Remember how that worked back in junior high? Now maybe it wasn't true for junior high guys, and maybe some junior high girls were able to rise above it all, but I know that around the eighth and ninth grades I began to care very much about what people thought of me. I worked very hard at picking out the right clothes. For the first time, I plucked by eyebrows, pierced my ears, put on makeup, bought platform shoes, and spent way too much time in front of the mirror. Not only was I trying to figure out who I was, but I wanted to make sure the image I chose would play well with my group of friends.

MySpace requires the same sort of forethought. Before MySpace users can become adept at networking, they need to have a profile that tells people about their likes, dislikes, interests, opinions, friends, and groups. It might be funny or vulgar; it all depends on how they want to come across. Profiles are easily updated, so interests and friends can change as quickly as one fad pops up and another dies out.

Signing Up

Starting a MySpace profile is easy. The first step involves registering as a MySpace user. Once a user name and password are determined, the most important task is creating a profile. MySpace screens will ask a number of questions, one of the first having to do with age. An interesting dilemma arises here. According to MySpace, users have to be at least fourteen years old. There is, of course, no good way to determine if someone is telling the truth, so savvy thirteen-year-olds simply lie about their age when they create their accounts. MySpace has also made it difficult for people to search for minors, so if users say they are eighteen or over, they can more easily be found by a lot of people looking for friends. Don't be surprised to find that age is routinely lied about on MySpace.

> PARENT TIP: Go to http://myspace.com and have a look. To access many of the site features, you will need to sign up and create a page yourself. Don't worry—you can leave it blank if you aren't willing to make a big commitment. Before you search for your child's site, consider asking for permission or, at the very least, give your child fair warning.

The next step is to come up with a screen name. Because the screen name shows up in many places, kids usually take time to craft just the right name that spells out just the right image. Unfortunately, many teens come up with screen names that do not communicate the wholesome image their parents hope for. "Hotbabe," "IWantYouNowGirl," and "imsosexxxy" are the kinds of names that may be funny when the teen first signs on but may draw the kind of attention that can get them into trouble.

> MAKE A CONNECTION: Ask your teen MySpacer about his or her sign-on name. Is it appropriate? Is it something that would be okay for a future employer to see? Is it something that may ask for unwanted attention? Does it give out too much information about your child's identity? What does it say about your child? Is it a good fit? These may be good questions to start a MySpace conversation with your teen.

Choosing a Picture

One of the first profile tasks involves choosing a picture. This step is not as easy as it seems. Teens don't just choose their school picture, because let's face it—that would be boring. They think about the mood they want to communicate. They think about how they want to come across, whether it be funny, sexy, tough, cute, serious, or something that people will talk about. If girls come across as sexy, they may get on a lot of boys' Top 8 lists (we'll talk about that one in a minute), but they will also get the attention of the wrong kind of people. If they want to come across as popular, they may include a picture with a lot of friends. If they want to come across as taken, they may include a picture with a boyfriend or girlfriend. If they are nervous about who will see them because their parents have talked to them about the dangers of putting out too much information, they may put up a picture of a pet or a flower. Pictures are easily switched as moods and interests change. And keep in mind, these pictures are important. They show up next to a teen's screen name on every profile of every one of their "friends." For many teens, it means their picture could be on hundreds or thousands of different MySpace pages.

MAKE A CONNECTION: **Ask to see your social networking teen's profile picture. Ask why he or she likes that picture and what it is intended to communicate.**

Filling in the Blanks

The next step in creating a MySpace profile involves answering the MySpace questions. These involve such deep issues as "about me," "interests," "people I'd like to meet," "favorite movies," "music," "television," and "heroes." As easy as these questions sound, I have to admit, it took me an embarrassingly long amount of time to fill these things out when I put together my MySpace page. For instance, I like a lot of movies, but I had to decide which ones sounded coolest or funniest or most "Peggy-ish." Once I put in my TV shows, I'd think of others that I liked better or other ones that just sounded better. I would think I had it down, and then I'd go to a friend's page and see better answers. I would quickly go back and change mine so they were just as funny or just as profound. Honestly, something that seems so silly and so straightforward as "my favorite food" quickly became an all-consuming search for the best way to communicate something funky about myself so that people I don't even know would say, "Oh, that Peggy, she is so funky!" *And I'm the one who keeps telling myself, I don't care what other people think!* Well, if you decide to try out the whole MySpace thing, you, too, may find that creating a profile takes you into a very odd, junior highish place where trying to find a voice and a unique way of expressing yourself is harder than you thought.

Once the MySpace profile blanks are filled in, the next step is to answer some multiple choice questions. These questions provide the basis for the search engines and help people get linked up on the basis of things like school, business, town, sexual orientation, or relationship status.

MAKE A CONNECTION: Ask how your MySpacing teen answered some of the "favorites" questions. You will undoubtedly get a kick out of how well you do or do not know your child.

Jazzing It Up

Whether or not you decide to try the whole MySpace thing, it's probably helpful to know how sophisticated MySpacers get so many cool things on their MySpace sites. Music, pictures, artwork, funky backgrounds, crawling banners, glittering headlines, and weird videos can all be used to customize MySpace sites to communicate a variety of things. Unfortunately, myspace.com is not terribly helpful in guiding newbie MySpacers in the creative aspects of developing a profile. Their suggestion is to find a MySpacer who knows more than you and have them lend you a hand. "It's a great way to get to know new people!" But if meeting new MySpace strangers is not high on your priority list, below are a few suggestions.

Music is an easy download away. You can create a MySpace site with music that automatically starts playing once users visit your site. Here is one way to easily accomplish that task. Find the MySpace site of a band or musician you enjoy. Most musicians have three or four music clips from their recent CD for people to listen to. Next to each of these files will be the word add. Click that button and the song will download to your site. Keep in mind that if the artist takes the file off his or her site, the link to your site will be broken and you will need to find a new song.

Creative background and formatting is another download away. One way to put pictures or backgrounds on your site is to find something on someone else's site that you like. If you move your cursor over the picture, it is quite likely a link will appear. You can then go to that website and download the things you want. You can also search the Web for "MySpace backgrounds" and find a number of websites willing to share with you free, fun things. Most sites will provide the download in the form of an HTML code that you copy and insert into one of the answer boxes in the profile creation section of your MySpace page. You "copy" the text in after the part where you put your favorite movie or television show. Keep in mind, in addition to the fun picture or background, the HTML code will also usually include advertisements or links to websites full of advertisements. So be aware of how the download looks on your site and what advertisements may be associated with the link.

PARENT TIP: **Here's a challenge: If you have decided to start a MySpace page, your best resource for how to do so is probably sitting in the family room watching TV. There is nothing more humbling for a parent and satisfying for a teen than to have the child teach the parent how to put cool things on MySpace.**

Hanging Out in the Space: The Art of Social Networking

Once the profile is created and the image is prepared, it is time to begin "hanging out." And hanging out doesn't just happen. Teenagers need skill and etiquette to know who to talk with and how to jump into a conversation. Whether talking next to the lockers or signing on to MySpace, the wise teen knows how to play the game, avoid the social missteps, and survive the often cruel and complex world of teenage socializing.

Making Friends

Before we go further, we need to define what a MySpace "friend" is. In case you think it has something to do with giving, sharing, and getting to know one another in a committed, long-lasting relationship, think again. A MySpace "friend" is a person who has access to your MySpace profile. His or her picture shows up in the "friends" section, and this person can read your blogs as well as comment on things he or she finds especially intriguing. For many MySpacers, being a friend has nothing to do with friendship but everything to do with being popular. Just as in instant messaging, the more friends on your list, the more popular you are perceived to be. The difference is that everyone in your social network gets to see how many MySpace friends you have.

I figured that even though having a lot of friends communicates popularity, everyone knows you can't have dozens of *real* friends, so who really cares how many MySpace friends you have? That was until a group of my senior communication students did a research project on the impact of a large friends list on Facebook. Boy, did I learn in a hurry what students thought about people with just a handful of online friends. If someone was given a Facebook profile of someone with a "small" number of friends and asked what they thought of that person, the Facebook person's perceived likeability and social attractiveness were significantly lower than for someone who had a lot of online friends on their list. Comments such as "What a loser," "I don't think this person would be a good friend," and "They need to get a life" were used to describe Facebookers with just a few friends. Keep in mind, students defined "a few friends" as *fifty*! That, of course, spurred me to get on my MySpace page and find some friends quickly, lest I became known as a loser. A funny thing happened a few weeks later when I was asked to be a friend by a dad from church who was trying to connect with his seventeen-year-old daughter by being a "cool dude" MySpacer. When I went on his MySpace page, I found me and one other person—and this dad was so happy to have two online friends! If he only knew.

The pressure to have lots of MySpace friends is pretty fierce. Just as with IM, friends are found and compiled in an effort to appear more popular. Some MySpacers even create programs that create lists of fake friends. They can buy preassembled friend lists, referred to as "whore lists," to bolster already bulging lists. One "legitimate" way to add a friend is to find the MySpace site of someone who is already known. This may be a real friend or a fine-looking *potential* friend from algebra class who is "the bomb." Once the potential friend has been identified, the first step is to search for that person's site. Searches are run by e-mail, school, town, screen name, or even the person's real name (while a user's real name can be used as a search term, it usually won't show up on the MySpace site for the viewing public to see).

If those strategies don't work, a person can also be found by zeroing in on his or her social network. For example, if you want to find Theresa's site, you can look at her boyfriend Jeremiah's site. A simple scroll through his list of friends will most likely display a picture of Theresa. With a quick click on the picture, her site will pop up. With another click on the "ask to be a friend" button on Theresa's profile, she will receive an e-mail with your friend request. Theresa can then thoughtfully contemplate whether she wants a new friend. Most often, the young person gets excited at the prospect of a new friend, forgoes the contemplation, and quickly accepts the person making the request into his or her social network.

But what if simple searches for individuals who are in a real-life social network isn't enough? No problem. You can do a little aggressive "friending." New friends can be found based on shared interests. Becoming part of a group means there are new people to meet who might be interested in talking about similar things. A look through friends' friend lists will provide new opportunities for expanded networks. With a little bit of work, you can be packin' a list of friends that is in the hundreds—even thousands.

Getting the scoop on potential friends is also a handy use of MySpace. Back in the olden days, all we could do to find out a little something about a cute girl or guy from gym class was to ask our friends. Well, that could be problematic, especially if the friend also thought the person from gym class was cute. But that would be no problem for today's high-tech teen. He or she could just look the person up on MySpace and learn about the person's character, interests, friends, and relationship status—everything a teen needs to know before making a move.

MAKE A CONNECTION: **Ask to take a look at your child's MySpace friends. You will undoubtedly see some nice-looking young people and some who seem way too "friendly." If there are some friends with suggestive or offensive pictures, talk to your child about what that communicates—both about the friend and about your child. Find out which friends are real friends and which ones are complete strangers, and ask your child to consider keeping his or her friend list limited to real-life acquaintances.**

Keeping Out Strangers

Making friends is what MySpace is all about. Unfortunately, when teens will do just about anything to get long friend lists, these "friends" may not be the kind of people you want your kids hanging out with. Always keep this balance in mind when using MySpace: on one side is meeting new people and having fun with the technology; on the other side is being safe and protecting private information. A more detailed discussion of safety and some of the dangers involved with MySpace will be covered in the following chapters. At this point, however, note that privacy settings can be put into place on MySpace. By choosing a more secure setting, MySpacers can restrict who has access to their site. The most commonly used privacy settings allow access to someone's profile only by people who have been accepted as "friends." These friends can view the teen's blogs, blog responses, pictures, videos, and any other personal information on the profile. They cannot, however, see the personal e-mails sent through MySpace or the bulletins sent by other friends. The user's name and e-mail are also usually hidden from public view.

Other privacy settings make it difficult for strangers to search for an individual without knowing his or her full name or e-mail address. If a user is under the age of eighteen, strangers will not be able to search for information using most of the regular search fields. While these privacy settings provide a certain degree of control and protection, they certainly are not foolproof. One of the problems is that teens will often let anyone be their "friend." That means a teen may have a full privacy setting but may also have strangers lurking in among their "friends," having full access to the teen's pictures and personal information. The other problem is that many teens choose not to use the privacy settings. They feel that the new and interesting people whom they would like to meet will not be able to find them if they increase their privacy settings. Furthermore, they will find it difficult to compile a big list of friends if they are hidden away behind security screens. Unfortunately for those teens who want to make their information less public, even the strictest security devices are no match for savvy MySpacers who really want to look at someone's profile.

MAKE A CONNECTION: **Talk to your MySpacer about privacy settings. Strongly consider requiring your child to use privacy settings, and encourage him or her to be choosy about who to approve as friends.**

Keeping Friends

Once you have established a nice list of friends, the next question is what do you do with them? This is the point at which most novice MySpacers throw up their hands in befuddlement. For almost a year, my Facebook site sat there reminding me of the very complex world of teenage connections that I just didn't "get." At first my students thought I was "something else" with my nifty Facebook page. I had funny answers to my favorite movies. I had a picture of my dog. Yep, they all wanted to be my friend. Soon I was basking in the glow of nearly twenty people who made up the "Dr. Kendall fan club." Clearly I was one of the most popular college professors around. After about a week or so, however, I couldn't help but notice . . . nothing happened. I would check my site, but it just sat there. I wondered whatever became of those great discussions and funny stories I had dreamed of sharing with my new "friends." After about seven months of nothing, I started bugging my students. "So, what *do* you actually do on Facebook?" I asked. "Do you just look at pictures? Where's the excitement? Where's that online rush? What am I missing?"

Eventually I started prying open the world of Facebook and MySpace drama. The lid came off when I was sitting at a diner sipping malts with four of my students at a conference in Indianapolis. There was clearly some tension at the table. One of my students explained about some drama happening back home on Facebook. The night before, my student's friend, let's call her Jill, was trying to get hold of her boyfriend. His Facebook site said he was online, but she sent messages with no response. Later that evening, she checked the site of another very cute young woman and found, to her horror, that her boyfriend had posted some fun little things on her site. The kicker was that the time stamp next to the posts was the exact same time she had been online waiting for his reply. Jill's boyfriend obviously had been flirting with this new girl instead of talking with his "real girlfriend"—and everyone in their social network knew it! And if that drama wasn't enough, one of my student's other friends had just gotten some truly thrilling news. The guy she has been dating for about two weeks had just changed his relationship status from "single" to "in a relationship"! All this excitement, and my poor students were stuck in a diner in Indianapolis, disconnected from the very real social happenings of their very social network.

MySpace and Facebook are clearly not the static media some would assume. Things are constantly changing. And with every change comes a bit of drama and a bit of teenage angst. There are two basic ways to be part of the social drama: put something on your site or put something on someone else's site. First, we'll discuss putting something on your own site. Every social networking site has space for its users to "blog" or write something that will be seen by everyone who peruses the page. These blogs take on different forms for different kinds of people. Some blogs are all about self-expression. I have seen blogs where users share in-depth thoughts about life. Young people who in the face-to-face world seem to be coping quite well with life feel free to share the real part of themselves online. These blogs can give true insight into what is important in a young person's life and what things have most recently captured their thinking. Unfortunately, these are also the type of blogs that most MySpacers and Facebookers admit they rarely read.

Other blogs are less about self-expression and more about social updates. Instead of telling each one of their friends about their vacations, blind dates, math tests, or the parties planned for Friday night, teenagers can just post the news up on their MySpace sites and know all their friends will see it. This is the type of blog that is usually short and sweet and read by social networkers who regularly check their friends' sites for just this kind of information. While some of this information is just plain information, some of it is packed with dramatic tension. For instance, a little hint that a teen may "like" someone is suddenly seen by an entire social network, including the target of the hinted-at "liking." If one teen is mad at another and says so on a blog, within minutes everyone knows about it. Blogging about everyday social matters is a quick way for teens to update all their friends about the little things that make up the drama of adolescence.

In addition to writing on their own sites, MySpacers can also post messages on other people's sites. Since these response messages are open for everyone to see, they tend to be quick little comments—usually things like "I love the picture" or "Miss you!" Unfortunately, if there is a feud between friends or social groups, some pretty nasty little comments can also show up for everyone to see. These comments are usually quickly removed by the person whose site got hit. If someone has more personal comments to make, he or she will usually use MySpace to send personal IMs or e-mails to friends. What starts on MySpace is often processed through IM, interplaying between the two technologies.

MAKE A CONNECTION: **Get permission to look through some of your MySpacer's blogs. You will undoubtedly see some deep aspects of your child that you hadn't known about before logging on. Look to see who comments most often on your child's page. This will give you a hint about which friends place great value in MySpace connections. You may also want to consider perusing some of your child's friends' sites–ask your child what he or she thinks about them. It may get you connected to the drama that is part of your teen's experience.**

Seeking Drama in the Space: The Art of Identifying Conflict

MySpace is a powerful medium through which many teenagers meet their important social needs. And, as you can imagine, MySpace often takes center stage in the inevitable teenage dramas that surround the whole process of "coming of age." If you find yourself the parent or adult friend of a MySpacer or of a teen who has MySpacing friends, there are three MySpace drama zones you will want to keep your ears and eyes open for—not just so you don't have to look like a "typical adult who doesn't understand this stuff," but because some of these things may seem silly but nevertheless carry a pretty significant emotional punch.

The Top 8

Can you imagine walking around school with a sign that says who your eight best friends are (and keep in mind that it also says who wasn't good enough to make your best friend list)? Think of how exciting it would be if you found out you just made the "Top 8" friend list of someone who was really popular. Think of how much it would hurt if someone who had been your best friend for a long time suddenly took your name off the list and replaced it with someone who was more popular or better looking. This drama plays out everyday on MySpace for everyone to see.[8]

MAKE A CONNECTION: **If your MySpacer is struggling with a friendship, keep an ear open for how MySpace may be involved. You may even want to ask if the friend is still on your child's Top 8. That piece of understanding could open up a whole world of hurt your child assumed you wouldn't understand.**

I'm not sure the creators of MySpace had this whole Top 8 thing in mind when they created the space, but there is one thing that logically happens when you have six hundred friends. Not all of them can show up on one page. To solve this dilemma, there is a spot for the top eight friends to appear on the main profile page, and the rest will show up on a scroll-down list. Keeping with teenage culture, this Top 8 list is not static. It changes according to who is cool, who is not cool, who is mad at whom, who likes whom, and, especially for teenage guys, who looks really hot. Changing the position of a friend or knocking a friend off the front page can be full of emotion and drama.

The Relationship Status Box

A second drama zone to watch out for is the all-important "relationship status" box. Yeah, you can imagine. What if the person you thought you were going out with suddenly changed his or her status to single? Virtual heads will roll. Want to break up with someone? Don't worry about that whole "Let's just be friends" talk. Just change your status box, and before you know it, your girlfriend or boyfriend will get the message along with every other friend across the country. Decided to take the relationship to the next level? No, it's not meeting the parents anymore. It's all about the MySpace relationship box. Drama, emotion, hope, disappointment, revenge, despair, opportunity—all these are wrapped up in a check-off box called relationship status.

Friendly Comments

A final drama zone where teenage MySpacers can feel a great amount of uncertainty and pain is in the blog comment section on a MySpace main page. As mentioned previously, teens often leave brief comments on each other's spaces. These comments are there for everyone in the teen's social network to see. Most of the time the comments are just little, noncommittal things that simply show that a friend has stopped by to say hi. Sometimes, however, these comments can be hurtful or embarrassing. Sometimes someone is just being mean on purpose. Other times a friend may not realize that what he or she has said doesn't feel good or isn't appropriate. That leaves the MySpacer with a dilemma: to delete or not to delete. What if the comment could get the teen in trouble? What if the comment was sent by someone who wasn't "cool"? What if the comment was something special left by a good friend who meant well but is just not jiving with the kind of image the teen is trying to portray? Deleting the comment of a friend can hurt. In many ways it is like hanging up on someone or turning around and walking away. But when it comes down to it, there are times in a teenager's life when image management is more important than keeping a friendship strong by leaving a MySpace comment untouched. This particular issue of what to do with friends' comments can be full of complex social intricacies.

MAKE A CONNECTION: **Try opening up a dialogue with your MySpacer about things that can make people mad on MySpace. Ask about how your teen has seen the "relationship status" box used, about the Top 8, and about people deleting other people's stuff. This might turn into an interesting conversation about your teen's friends and frustrations.**

MySpace is a big, complex, often overwhelming piece of online communication technology—especially for parents who are trying to figure out what their kids are up to. While it provides a high-tech equivalent to the hangout spaces of our day, it also carries with it some very particular challenges and dangers. That is why it is so essential for parents to try it out.

Sometimes I find MySpace confusing and feel as if I will never understand how it so powerfully pulls young users to its sign-in page. Other times I find it offensive and wish kids would find a more wholesome way to connect with each other. But one thing I know: kids are using MySpace to meet a lot of needs, and they are often doing it alone. Can you imagine what the junior high lockers would be like if every kid there knew there were no adults in sight and, in fact, they knew that most adults were too overwhelmed to even come into the building? Social networking would undoubtedly take on a much harsher, less controlled, more dangerous edge. If you have kids or know of kids who are on MySpace, have the courage to figure out how to "enter the building." Figure out how to come alongside your teen, helping him or her manage the many challenges and pitfalls of growing up in a very high-tech world.

The following chapters are designed to present a balanced perspective of the good and bad things associated with online technology like MySpace and instant messaging. As Christian parents, it is important that we figure out the best way to protect our kids from the very deep-seated evil in this world while preparing them to successfully operate in a high-tech culture. That balancing act is not easy, but it is one to which God has called us and one for which God has provided us with courage, understanding, and patience. The next chapter will examine the positive things about online communication technology, including the reasons kids like it so much and the needs the technology is helping high-tech teens meet. The following chapters will then look at some of the negative things that can trap and hurt kids who live too much of their lives in a virtual world.

MySpace Discussion Starters

MySpace history. Ask your teen if he or she sees MySpace as the "unbridled West" of cyberspace.

MySpace alternatives. Talk with your teen about considering other social networking sites.

MySpace profile. Ask for permission to see your teen's site.

MySpace picture. Ask to see your teen's profile picture. Ask why he or she chose that one.

MySpace adventure. Try out MySpace, putting together your own profile. Ask for your teen's help.

MySpace friends. Look together at some of your teen's friends' pictures. Talk about what the pictures communicate.

MySpace privacy. Talk about the value of privacy settings and being choosy about new "friends."

MySpace blogging. Ask to see one of your teen's best blogs. Try blogging for yourself.

MySpace drama. Talk about your teen's Top 8 friends. Ask when he or she changes things around.

the good
"Why Do My Kids Like the Computer More Than Me?"

It was a hot, sunny day in Florida when I first began to feel as if something was taking my place. That something had wires, a fancy keyboard, and a slick, collapsible screen. All I had were overcooked chicken nuggets, an outdated swimsuit, and sunglasses that I should have thrown out in the eighties. We were on a family vacation at our favorite spot. We had gone to all the attractions, eaten at our favorite places, and swum in our favorite pool. Sure, the kids had fun. They laughed at some of my jokes and put on a "good face" when brightly dressed, gigantic cartoon characters came to our table to give them a kiss on the head. But something was missing. They seemed a little bored with their parents. Their conversations weren't as energetic and happy as when they were seven or eight years old. They didn't sing along with "It's a Small World" and seemed a little embarrassed as their mother skipped down the sidewalk trying to get all the words to "Seventy-six Trombones" and "Shipoopee."

The real lesson came when we found out the wireless connection in the hotel worked with our computer. There was such relief, such joy on their faces as they logged on for a quick update with their friends. They weren't online long, but there was a clear sense of satisfaction at dinner that night. The message was clear: they loved their parents and always would, but they *really liked* their technology and the way it let them connect with their friends.

As teenagers travel through their adolescent years, a lot of things happen. They begin to disengage from parents, establishing their own sense of who they are and how they fit into a broader culture. Much of this work is done in their social circles. They watch how other people act and how other people treat them. They watch for cues as to what others perceive them to be good at and what others seem to expect of them. They experiment and find out what works in relationships and what hurts. They talk with others to find out what their faith really means and how it can uniquely play out in their lives.

While some of these lessons may be taught by wise parents, most lessons are learned in settings where they hang out with their friends. And whether we like it or not, the place they hang out with their friends is often found online. What that means is that technology is helping them accomplish the tasks of adolescence. And in some cases, technology is actually helping them accomplish these tasks in ways that are more effective than what would be the case in traditional, face-to-face settings. It is valuable to look at some of the positive things about kids using IM and MySpace, especially as they relate to friendships, identity, and faith. As we seek to protect our children from the dangers of technology, we can't forget that there are plenty of good reasons why kids love their technology so much. Some of those reasons might actually be helping them grow into mature, strong Christian young people.

Building Friendships: Keeping the Connection Open

Connections Made Fun

In talking with hundreds of middle school, high school, and college students about online communication technology, one thing came across loud and clear: they love their technology! They love to sit and IM with friends. They love to mess around with their MySpace profile. They love to read about what's new with their friends. They love to share memories, pictures, homework tips, music, videos, website links, and games. Technology just seems to put a zip into the lives of young people.

According to a number of IMers, the computer makes hanging out together fun. "It gives me some relaxing time chatting with friends about the outdoors, sports scores, news, and just joking around," says one student. "You are able to talk to people just for fun, not having to call them and make a big effort to talk to them." And who wouldn't rather sit and do homework with a bunch of friends? According to happy IMers, there is nothing better than to sit with a math book on one side of the desk and instant messaging on the other. When math problems get confusing, a team of friends from class is online, probably doing the same thing. It's easy to ask about an assignment that doesn't make sense or get the notes from a class they missed. Group work is much easier when they don't have to figure out rides and times to meet between their very busy schedules. Many IMers say doing homework together is what they like best about instant messaging.

MAKE A CONNECTION: **Ask your child what is most fun about IM. Ask to see some of the fun things he or she does on IM, or maybe even ask for a demonstration of how to play a game. Your child might really enjoy showing off!**

Having IM around also seems to make other tasks more enjoyable. Because connecting on the computer is all about multitasking, IMing can easily be done while watching TV, cleaning a room, or listening to music. Online gaming has become an incredibly popular way for young people to spend time with their "friends." According to the 2005 Pew Internet and American Life Project, nearly 81 percent of teen Internet users play games online. That represents about 17 million people and signifies growth of 52 percent in the number of online gamers since 2000.[1] A little game play, a little conversation, a little joke telling, a little play—this is all part of hanging out and having a good time with friends, using the Internet to provide the connection that isn't possible when a busy mom or dad doesn't have time to drive a teen over to a friend's house for an afternoon. From a student perspective, one of the greatest benefits of online communication technology is that, plain and simple, it's fun.

Connections Made Easy

A second benefit identified by teenage users of IM and social networking is that the sites help keep them connected with their friends. Most of the people with whom teenagers communicate through IM and MySpace are not creepy strangers, but friends from their everyday social network, including the kids they hang out with at school. When IMers can keep in touch through IM, they are able to keep those relationships fresh and growing. It is no surprise that a majority of surveyed teenage IMers report feeling closer to friends with whom they IM than with those they do not. The technology allows them to keep the connection open—to find out how a friend's day went or how a math test went, or whether they talked to a cute girl or cute guy at lunch. It keeps them involved in the lives of their friends and builds a foundation for positive face-to-face relationships.

New friends. Instant messaging and social networking sites also make it easy to get to know new people. Some of these may be people the teen has recently met in the real world. In real life, getting to know a new person often takes awhile, because we have to wait until we bump into each other again. Many times that never happens. However, when teens are connected online, they can be more proactive about building friendships.

MySpace and sites like it can provide helpful background in getting to know someone. It can provide a good idea of what interests are shared so that the teens know what topics of conversation might work best. It also provides a neutral meeting place where simple topics can be talked about, such as the music or the pictures on someone's site. And instant messaging can help "grease the wheels" in a new relationship. It is much less awkward to have a conversation with a new person online than if the two teens were standing there looking at each other and feeling uncomfortable and tongue-tied. Once that basic relationship is built, face-to-face meetings will be much more comfortable and natural. This new way of getting around those old feelings of awkwardness might actually help build the confidence of teens, encouraging them to get to know more people and make more new friends.

Technology also makes it easier to get to know people who will never be met in the real world. As potentially risky as meeting strangers is, there are also some benefits in getting to know people with similar interests and beliefs. One of the strengths of MySpace is how it builds connections. If people are interested in the same kind of music, they can get together and talk about it. If they are interested in cooking, drama, even Christianity, they can find other people who can relate and add insight and virtual friendship. In all likelihood, it doesn't involve meeting in dark alleys, running away to foreign countries, or being stalked on the way home from school. Most of these connections are simple conversations with interesting people. After all, we can learn a lot from people we may never meet. We can also gain support from people who have similar experiences. Online support groups have existed for a number of years and provide a unique way for individuals to gain information along with real emotional support. As long as teens understand the dangers of building relationships with strangers, there are clearly some relational benefits to glean from social networking.

Old friends. Another way online communication helps build relationships is in the way it keeps people connected even though they may not be physically close. According to the 2005 Pew Internet and American Life Project, 90 percent of teenage IMers use IM to keep in touch with someone in a different state.[2] Whether connecting with a parent who is out of town for work or a friend who has moved across the country, IM makes long-distance relationships more likely and easier to be maintained. A friend of mine has a daughter who is a full-time missionary in the Philippines. It was pretty tough at first, but they soon figured out a time when they could both be online. "It's like sitting with my daughter, having coffee," my friend told me. "She tells me about her day, while I sip my morning joe. It's not quite like having her here, but it sure makes her being there a lot easier."

Many of my college students are able to keep up with their friends from high school even though they may not live in the same town anymore. This is a distinct change from a few years ago when the only time high school friends could connect was when they returned to their hometown at Christmas and Easter. My students talk about how, even though IM is not quite the same as being together, it keeps communication going so that when they do get together, they don't have to spend so much time getting caught up. Other students describe relationships from camp or missions trips that keep them going throughout the year. While their friends at home may not be a great influence on them, through IM they are able to keep a spiritual connection going with friends with whom they have shared some deep faith experiences. In many ways, IM opens up long-distance relationships to help fill the void many teens feel in their everyday relationships at school and at work.

PARENT TIP: **If you or another relative or adult travels out of town, try using IM to connect with each other. Your child may get a kick out of it, and you may begin to see why the technology can be so addictive!**

Connections Made Deep

Instant messaging and social networking sites allow teens to build and maintain connections that are both fun and easy. They can also create connections that are quite deep and meaningful. One of the unique aspects of online communication is that it tends to encourage "hyperpersonal" communication. While this concept will be discussed more fully in the following chapter, it should be kept in mind that a technology that helps a teenager articulate complex emotions and pain can be quite beneficial.

Let's face it: being a teenager can be rough. There are a lot of stresses associated with growing up and trying to fit in. There are also a lot of stresses associated with growing up in this fast-paced, superficial culture we live in. Being a teenager today is different than being a teenager twenty years ago. Today's teens are faced with temptations and challenges we will never know about. It is vital that young people be able to process those temptations, unpacking which claims are true and which ones are lies, which values are good and which ones are bad. It is also a crucial time for them to figure out which parts of their parents' faith they will abandon and which parts they will assimilate into their own lives.

Unfortunately, there aren't many places teens feel comfortable talking about deeply personal things. One of the things that IM and social networking technology does is provide that kind of place. Many young people are much more willing to work through complex emotions over the computer than in face-to-face situations. The virtual world seems to provide a safe and comfortable place for them to be honest with each other. Surveyed teenage IMers were quite vocal about how great it was to have a space where it was okay to open up and be "real." For instance, one young woman talked about how it was easier for her to tell her friends how much they meant to her online, because face-to-face it would be "just too weird." Topics that are personal and significant but hard to talk about seem to come out easier when friends are online. "It allowed me to share my faith in a good way," offered another young IMer. "I'm not very good at speaking my mind or beliefs, so, in typing them . . . I could get my words on 'paper' before actually sharing them."

These meaningful interactions can also turn into significant helping experiences. Because IM allows friends to "be there" when they are most needed, intimate and opportune conversations take place online. A number of students recounted times when they were able to help their friends through difficult circumstances, some of them very time-sensitive in nature. "I remember talking to a suicidal friend online," shares one student. "I think I may have saved her life. I'm really glad I was there." Clearly, the private nature of IM carries with it some perceived value on the part of teenage IMers.

MAKE A CONNECTION: **Ask if your IMer thinks it is easier to be honest and personal online than in real life. Talk about why he or she thinks that is.**

When I look at how my kids use instant messaging, I am humbled at how much better they are at building and maintaining their friendships than I am. As life gets busy, good friendships become that much more valuable. Instant messaging and sites like MySpace can help teenagers build strong relationships that allow them to navigate through some of the tough areas of adolescence.

Building Identity: Expressing an Emerging Personality

Besides allowing young people to enhance relationships, another role communication technology plays is giving them a way to express themselves. In light of the developmental tasks involved with establishing a unique identity, it isn't surprising that teens appreciate the way online communication technology helps them build confidence and an ability to express their newly emerging personality.

Confidence Builders

If you have recently passed by the middle school youth room at church, you may have seen a group of loud, rowdy kids flying around the room, laughing, having a good time, and one or two quiet kids standing in the corner just watching. It's pretty painful to imagine what is running through the quiet kids' minds. They might be thinking that no one likes them or wishing that they fit in better. At the very least, they probably wished they had the confidence or the social skills to join in. One of the great benefits of technology like instant messaging, especially for kids who tend to be fairly quiet, is that it allows them to build their skills and their confidence in a relatively safe environment.

When teens engage in online conversations, they can control many of the things that tend to create stress in face-to-face situations. They can think about what they are going to say before they say it. They can craft each word and each sentence so it comes across just right. They don't have to feel rushed or awkward, as IM conversations don't have the same rhythm as face-to-face conversations. Conversations are often about simple topics and are easy to start and easy to leave. And, maybe best of all, they don't have to worry about seeing someone give them a dirty look or a roll of their eyes. Instant messaging provides the type of conversational environment that can help shy, quiet, or unconfident kids develop interactional skills. It can feel like a nice first step. And once the initial relationships are developed, it is much easier to engage in face-to-face conversations.

MAKE A CONNECTION: **Ask if your IMer feels more confident online. Ask how that, in turn, impacts how he or she acts. This is a great conversation starter to get teens talking about how IM impacts them.**

Bridge Builders

In addition to helping kids feel more confident about themselves and more comfortable in social situations, IM can also help teens develop relationships with people who are not in their social group. For my kids it started happening in sixth or seventh grade. They started realizing the opposite sex was different than they were. They suddenly became unable to talk with kids of the opposite sex whom they had known and played with for years, because someone might think they were "in love or something." Studies show that teens begin using instant messaging when they are in sixth or seventh grade. Interestingly, the biggest gender lag is in sixth grade where 44 percent of sixth grade boys regularly go online compared to 79 percent of sixth grade girls. By eighth grade, however, both boys and girls are actively using the computer to talk with their friends.[3]

It is among this awkward age group that I have seen some fascinating social uses of instant messaging. IM allows middle schoolers to bridge the gap between the newly created, gender-based social groups. It lets boys and girls talk to each other in ways that are natural and comfortable—out of the purview of friends or parents who would see nothing wrong with making a big deal of an innocent conversation. In one middle school classroom, I found that most of the girls instant messaged most of the guys, building good friendships with each other. They said, however, that they almost never talked to each other at school and they would never let their friends know who they were IMing.

Instant messaging can also help young people develop relationships with people who are different or who are not accepted by those in their face-to-face social group. IM can help young people learn how to talk with people they don't usually hang out with in a way that enhances relationships and builds bridges, whether it be boys talking with girls, popular kids talking with unpopular kids, or kids from one clique talking with those from another. This, in turn, can help lay the foundation for partnerships or understanding that may not be available in real contexts.

MAKE A CONNECTION: **Ask if your IMer sends instant messages to people he or she probably would not talk to at school. Think about challenging your child to reach out to quiet or less popular kids on IM.**

Identity Builders

Whether helping students be proactive about making new friends or helping them gain the confidence and skills necessary to build those friendships, instant messaging can be a useful tool to aid teens in accomplishing some of the tasks that facilitate social development. Tools like MySpace can also assist older teens in learning how to express themselves in ways that help them sort out and establish their emerging identities and personalities.

When asked why they like sites such as MySpace and Facebook, most teens mentioned how nice it was to be able to "express" themselves. One youth pastor I recently interviewed said he regularly uses his MySpace site to showcase his kids' creativity. MySpace provides space where teens can try out their artistry, poetry, song writing, musicianship, and filmmaking, and get feedback. There are few other places where students have the opportunity or the will to show off their talent like they do on MySpace.

In addition to allowing teens to express their talents, social networking also lets kids express their hearts. It is a forum where they can talk about what bugs them or what excites them. By reading their blogs, you can get a very personal glimpse of what is important to a young person. You can see the kinds of ideas that have captured their thinking, whether political, religious, sexual, cultural, or social. While not every MySpacer uses this forum as a place to deepen or clarify their thinking, most do use it to express some aspect of their personalities. Most MySpacers are very intentional about what pictures, music, background designs, and favorites lists they put on their sites. There is a certain amount of polishing, tweaking, and experimenting that goes on with what ends up on a MySpace site, because it so distinctly says something about the kind of person the teen wants to be. Self-expression is therefore clearly a positive aspect of online technology that assists teens in designing the identities they hope to adopt.

MAKE A CONNECTION: **Ask your MySpacer to share with you the best thing about his or her site–get your child to show off a little. This may be the encouragement your child needs to allow you access into his or her emerging identity.**

Building Christian Relationships: Using Technology to Foster Faith

Part of my research on online communication technology has focused on how youth pastors use the technology to enrich the work they do with young people. (For more information, see the related book, *Rewired: Youth Ministry in an Age of IM and MySpace,* also published by Judson Press, 2007.) The impetus for the original study came from a student of mine who was working as a middle school youth pastor. It wasn't long before she found that by connecting with her kids through technology, she was able to touch their hearts in a way that was very different from anything else she had tried. She found that kids were especially open to talking about weighty topics online. She also found that the computer allowed her to communicate the love of Christ in ways that resonated with her middle school kids. The lesson for me, as a mom, is that while technology may lead kids to temptation and sin, it can also lead them to a deeper and more committed understanding of who they are in Christ. This understanding can occur when they use the technology to search for information concerning faith, when they use it to talk about and process their faith, and when they use it to proclaim their faith.

Searching for the Gospel

One of the people I have gotten to know through the research I have done with MySpace is a youth pastor named John. He is passionate about reaching kids for Christ, and it shows in everything he does. Once he gets talking about the vision he has for using the Internet to share the gospel with young people, there is no stopping him. Instead of taking the perspective that most of us would take, seeing all the problems with MySpace and all the possible ways his kids could get into trouble, John saw potential. He saw a place where the love of Christ and the power of the gospel could shine much brighter and much deeper for young people than it could during the Sunday service where his kids usually sat fooling around in the back of the sanctuary, listening to music and sermons that rarely touched their hearts and souls.

So John set about creating a MySpace site that would introduce the gospel in terms his kids understood, using the technology they enjoyed. He put up information about himself, music from the newest Christian rock bands, and links to fun games and clean Internet sites. He uploaded videos that powerfully presented the gospel through stories of Jesus' life or of the end times. He put up blogs that dealt with issues his Christian kids were dealing with, including Christian perspectives on dating, sex, friendship, parents, self-image, and more. He posted the notes from his weekly Bible study along with songs, poetry, and videos his kids created especially for his site.

Then something amazing happened. God showed up on MySpace. Not only were the kids from his youth group linked to his site, but through the magic of social networking technology, each of his kids' five or six hundred friends were suddenly one click away from the gospel message, presented in fun and accessible ways. John soon was receiving messages from young people he had never met. They had linked to his site through a friend, had listened to the music, watched the videos, and read about Christianity. Since they didn't really know any other Christians, they found John on MySpace and asked him questions—important questions, tough questions, the kinds of questions that would rarely come up if they were in a face-to-face context. He found that kids were able to access the gospel message in a nonthreatening environment and process it in their own way and in their own time. MySpace became an avenue through which John could reach kids who might never come to a youth group meeting or a Sunday service but were willing to visit his MySpace page.

MAKE A CONNECTION: **Sit with your teen and search MySpace for youth pastor sites, Christian band sites, or other places that share the gospel. Ask your teen to point out what on those sites is appealing and what is a turnoff.**

Processing the Gospel

Social networking is not the only tool that can help young people connect with the gospel message. While sites like MySpace may provide young people with information about faith, instant messaging allows them to process what they are thinking. Instant messaging gives teens who are struggling with who they are and how their faith fits into their lives a safe place to ask questions.

Take the case of Jeff.[4] Jeff is a youth pastor who routinely checks the MySpace sites of the kids he works with. One day he found some particularly disturbing things on the site of a young man named Sid, a student he had been working with for quite some time. Sid often came to youth group events but never seemed terribly engaged. It was clear that he felt awkward coming into church with his baggy pants, multiple piercings, and thick, silver chains, but his parents insisted Sid join them at church on Sunday mornings. Jeff had begun to start a good dialogue with Sid through instant messaging and MySpace. Every now and then they would post things on each other's MySpace pages, share music files, and talk about school and girls and whatever else came up.

One evening as Jeff was looking through MySpace, he found himself captured by Sid's site. He had posted a long blog that reeked of depression and suicide. It was surely a cry for help. Jeff quickly turned on his instant messaging and connected with Sid. As Jeff prayed through every IM message that appeared on the screen, Sid began to open up in ways that were honest and full of raw emotion. Jeff was able to point him toward the Savior in a way that touched the hurting young man's heart. As they signed off, they set up a time the next day when they could both sit down and talk to Sid's parents. MySpace allowed Sid to ask for help in a nonthreatening manner—it didn't require that he call someone or go up to someone at church where everyone could see. Instant messaging allowed Sid to open up and work through very difficult and confusing emotions in a way that felt safe. IM and MySpace allowed Jeff to be there right when Sid needed him.

Youth pastors aren't the only ones to use instant messaging to help young people process what it means to be a Christian teenager in today's culture. Many of the teens I interviewed said they have talked with their friends about spiritual things using instant messaging. Whether they are supporting others, saying that they are praying for them, or giving godly counsel, young people use online communication technology to talk about things they may not normally address in face-to-face contexts.

MAKE A CONNECTION: **Ask if your teen ever talks about his or her faith on instant messaging. If the answer is no, ask why not. If the answer is yes, ask what it was like–if it was easier than doing so in a face-to-face conversation with the person.**

Experiencing the Gospel

In addition to providing a place to process the gospel, IM and social networking sites allow Christian teens to connect, to support each other, and to partake in many of the same things found in a traditional, face-to-face Christian community. Back in the old days, Christian community was built on hot dishes and home Bible studies. Today teens have created Christian communities based on instant messages, MySpace bulletins, and virtual Bible studies. Kids who commit to coming together to build each other up in their faith use things like instant messages to check in with one another and to encourage and pray for one another. MySpace blogs are a way of processing a Scripture passage or talking about the Bible study message from youth group that week. One youth pastor says that IM and MySpace have helped him create a small group of dynamic young Christians committed to holding each other accountable. While these small groups look a little different than what we had when we were in high school, they are a tool God is using in the lives of today's Christian young people.

PARENT TIP: **Do an online search to find a Christian community or online church. Poke around to see if you can figure out why online worship and community building can be so powerful and inviting.**

Proclaiming the Gospel

Some of the most powerful and moving stories I have heard about IM and MySpace center on teens using these tools to proclaim the gospel of Jesus Christ. Take, for example, the story of Jenna, a new Christian who has experienced God transforming the way she sees and responds to things. She is getting along better with her parents, she has found some new friends at school who are a better influence on her, and she has even started going to church. The thing that strikes me about Jenna is that she is deeply in love with Jesus Christ. She is excited about her walk with him and wants everyone to know it. Her energy spilled over as she talked about how she sat down one day with her youth pastor and some friends from church to talk strategy. She wanted her friends to come to Christ, and she felt that IM and MySpace were two ways to introduce them to Christ.

As a group, they talked about how they could communicate the love of Christ through the technology they were already using on a day-to-day basis. The first thing they did was to commit to each other that their MySpace pages would always be honoring to God. That meant they had to be vigilant about taking off friends who had raunchy pictures or comments that weren't positive and uplifting. The second thing they committed to do was to add things to their MySpace sites that would communicate the gospel. Jenna decided to add Christian music to her site, put some poetry she had written up on her profile that described what her faith meant to her, and even highlighted a link to an Internet site that clearly explained the gospel. The next thing the group did was figure out how to encourage their non-Christian friends. They decided to regularly go through their friend lists, pray for each person, and send them notes of encouragement through MySpace e-mail. Over the next few months, this group of young people helped keep each other accountable while they made their IM and MySpace sites places that communicated who they were in Christ.

MAKE A CONNECTION: **Ask if your teen feels his or her MySpace site is consistent with who he or she is at school, at church, and at home. Ask what your teen thinks about kids who put things about their faith on their MySpace sites.**

God can use online communication technology—from a youth leader's encouraging instant messages to a teenager's creative MySpace site—in ways that bring young people closer to himself. As we contemplate what communication technology is, how it is impacting our children, and what role it should play in our households, we can too easily overlook the positive things it has to offer our young people. There is a reason our kids like this technology so much, and we owe it to them to consider the good things it has to offer. Whether helping young people to be more committed friends, to express themselves more confidently and creatively, or to better understand what it means to be a Christian, technology like IM and MySpace aid them in conquering some of the challenges of growing up in this high-tech world.

"The Good" Discussion Starters

Instant Messaging

Ask why your teen thinks IM is a good thing.

Ask your teen if it is easier to be totally honest online than in person. Why?

Ask your teen how he or she is different online.

Ask if your teen IMs kids that he or she doesn't usually hang out with at school or elsewhere.

Challenge your teen to connect with less popular or quiet kids with IM.

Try out instant messaging. Find a buddy and sign on!

MySpace

Ask your teen to name the best thing he or she has ever put on MySpace.

Search with your teen for Christian bands and youth pastor sites. What does he or she like? What is too corny?

Ask if your teen has ever talked about his or her faith on MySpace or IM. What was it like?

Ask if your teen thinks his or her own site (or other friends' sites) are consistent with who the users are in real life.

the bad

"If It Isn't Real, How Can It Hurt So Much?"

Kids love their online technology. And a lot of good things come with the flickering screen, the clicking keyboard, and the overused Internet connection. Being optimistic and hopeful about the benefits technology has to offer is extremely important when we talk with our kids about instant messaging and MySpace. However, to serve the best interests of our children as we protect them and equip them to function and even flourish in a high-tech culture, we need to come to terms with the many negative aspects of online communication technology. This chapter will lay the groundwork for a discussion of how technology is fundamentally impacting the way our kids think and behave. The following chapter will go on to discuss specific ways we parents can come alongside our kids to help them survive and thrive in this changing and confusing world.

Let's begin with a look at how the heavy use of online communication can change the way young people think. The example of Jesse, a ninth grade girl, illustrates the fundamental problem. Imagine yourself peeking over the shoulder of this young woman who is sitting in her bedroom late one night feeling all alone. She has never gone on a date and never been kissed, and she wonders if any-one could ever love her. Not knowing where else to turn, she clicks on her computer. Soon the warm glow of the screen fills her mind with feelings of richness and connection. Scrolling down her buddy list, she notices "Johnboy," a guy she knows from math class. Even though she doesn't know him well, he seems like a nice guy. He strikes her as being the kind of person who is a good listener and a good friend—just the sort of guy Jesse needs. She sends him an IM greeting, and a quick "hey, Jesse" pops up on his screen. It isn't long before small talk turns into deep sharing as Jesse explores with John some of her deepest feelings about how depressed she feels and how sometimes it seems like no one really loves her.

"It feels so good to get those thoughts out," thinks Jesse. "And I can tell he cares about me—just by the little comments and sad faces he sends." It helps to have such a good friend. With that she sighs, says good night, slips into bed, and thinks about how lucky she is and what a great couple she and John would make. As John signs off, he flips back to the two other conversations he is having with his friends.

"You wouldn't believe this girl!" types John. "She has some major problems—just the kind of girl you guys should go out with!!" With that, John goes to his MySpace page and writes a poem about "weird Jesse" that is soon downloaded by all their friends.

Jesse was looking for a connection. When she went to the computer to find that connection, she thought she had found the relationship she was looking for. The problem? The relationship wasn't real. When teens routinely operate in a world of digital relationships, reality can inadvertently become merged with make-believe. An understanding of self and others that is grounded in *real-life* interactions may slowly be replaced with more convenient interpretations grounded in *virtual* interactions. Make no mistake: relationships built over IM and MySpace can be every bit as real to a young person as the relationships they form in school or at church. In fact, many of the same relationships are managed in both realms. And don't forget, there are a lot of good things technology can add to those relationships.

Unfortunately, online communication technology can also create the *appearance* of relationship, connection, and shared meaning where none truly exists.

It is crucial for young people to be able to identify times when virtual reality begins to mask true reality. As parents, we need to be aware of this balance between real and virtual so we can help our teens navigate the distorted reality created by online communication technology. Three areas of concern include how virtual reality impacts understanding and relationships, community and responsibility, and an understanding of who God is and how he works in our lives.

Missing the Understanding, Missing the Relationship

One key to successful relationships is an ability to share with one another. As friendships grow, trust is developed and friends cultivate an ability to "read" one another—they get good at understanding what the other person is experiencing. Unfortunately, one of the biggest headaches young people report with IM and other online communication technologies is the ongoing issue of misunderstanding.

Missing the Nonverbals

When a conversation full of smirks, grimaces, smiles, frowns, yells, hesitations, energy, and silence is replaced with nothing but text, meaning gets lost. Recall Jesse's IM conversation with John. That particular interaction was filled with a boatload of misunderstanding. If she and John had been sitting in the same room, Jesse quickly would have picked up that John was not interested. And if for some reason that starry-eyed, teenage crush got in the way of Jesse seeing what was really going on, John certainly would sense something was wrong as Jesse gazed at him a bit more intently, smiled a bit more broadly, giggled a bit more loudly, and snuggled a bit more closely. Instead, all those nonverbals were lost as the messages traveled through the computer lines, being replaced with one-way thoughts of love and romance. Once nonverbal cues are removed from a conversation, there is much more ambiguity.

According to communication scholars, most of the information we get about our relationships comes in the form of nonverbal cues. For instance, by watching how Andre looks at us, we can tell how much respect he has for us. By listening to Deanna's voice, we can tell how important something is to her. By leaning over and hugging someone, we can share a deep bond of commitment. Without these cues, an important part of understanding gets lost, and much of that understanding comments on how the relationship is going—what the other person thinks of us and what he or she thinks of what we're saying. The result is that we are left to fill in the blanks. *The problem arises when we fill in the blanks with things we expect or hope for instead of things that really exist.*

Misinterpreting the Messages

So, what are the implications of this natural tendency to "fill in the blanks"? The most obvious result is that teens will have misunderstandings with their friends. They expect it. In fact, many surveyed teens report that they just don't take things too seriously when they are said online. Experience has taught them that there is always the possibility of reading a message in the wrong way or even that a message is coming from someone pretending to be someone else. According to these teens, snotty comments or brash remarks just can't be taken too personally.

From these comments, one might assume that misunderstanding stemming from digital conversations simply isn't that big of a deal because teens regularly sort through conversations with a skeptical eye. If you are a parent of a teenager who has spent time online, however, you know this tendency toward skepticism is not always operating the way it should. Certainly, online users may know in their heads that a hurtful comment is probably nothing but a misunderstanding. Feeling that ambiguity in their hearts, however, may be much more difficult.

When it comes right down to it, teens have just as much difficulty as the rest of us identifying when an ambiguous comment should be interpreted in a positive or negative way. It is much easier to interpret messages in ways that are consistent with how we see ourselves and how we see our relationships. For instance, if a teen is already working with a low self-concept, it is certainly easier and more consistent with his or her worldview to interpret an ambiguous comment as negative. If a friend is already ticked off at another friend, it is much easier to interpret an innocent comment as a personal attack. Misunderstanding of what is said and how it is said is a natural consequence of our tendency to "fill in the blanks."

MAKE A CONNECTION: **Talk to your teen about times he or she has had misunderstandings because of something said online. Ask how it was misinterpreted and how your child eventually figured it out. This conversation may help your teen better understand the possibility of multiple interpretations the next time an online buddy makes a harsh comment that takes him or her by surprise.**

Redefining Relationships

Another consequence of "filling in the blanks" has to do with how relationships are developed and defined. When young people build relationships online, it's not hard for reality to become blurred with fantasy. Relationships may become more about what the teen needs rather than what truly exists. For instance, romances seem to flourish in online environments. If a teen wants a girlfriend or boyfriend badly enough, he or she can blissfully assume the person on the other end of the computer is also "interested." Suddenly, sweet smiles, flirtatious winks, and loving glances are read between every line of text. Quite honestly, teenage infatuation is rarely grounded in reality. However, technology can certainly make relationships with the opposite sex even more complex and more open to misinterpretation and misunderstanding.

Friendships can also be misinterpreted. If a teen is feeling lonely or disconnected, he or she may readily interpret simple, polite IM conversations or blog postings as indications of trust and commitment. As a result, very personal thoughts and feelings may be shared with others who are not trustworthy and who may end up betraying that trust. Without the nonverbal information, it is easy to lose the ability to truly connect and accurately interpret the response of the other. This, in turn, certainly complicates and potentially compromises teenage relationships.

MAKE A CONNECTION: **If your teen is dating someone, you may want to ask how much time he or she spends online with that special friend. Encouraging the couple to spend less time online and more time face-to-face may help them more accurately define their relationship, keeping fantasy romance in line with reality.**

Forging Intimacy

A third consequence of "filling in the blanks" has to do with a tendency of online technology to stimulate something communication scholars refer to as "hyperpersonal communication." Think back to Jesse. As she is sitting in her room on her computer, her mom and dad having long since gone to bed, her soulful songs play on her iPod as she writes some deeply felt poetry that describes the teenage angst she is feeling about growing up. She struggles with who she is, who God is, and where her place is in this world. It is only natural for her to post her poetry on her MySpace site since it so beautifully communicates something about her inner soul. It's easy for her to imagine others coming to her site and being inspired and touched by her moving and deeply personal thoughts. The IM conversations she shares with her friends continue this idealized version of intimacy and closeness as she types into the night.

Will Jesse's friends ever actually read her lengthy MySpace blog? Probably not. Are her IM friends actually listening with heartfelt caring and empathy, connecting like true friends with true shared meaning as they also multitask in multiple conversations with three or four other friends? Probably not. But Jesse feels as if she is in an intimate setting with a trusted friend whom she has envisioned sitting there nodding and emotionally making the connection. It is not surprising that she would feel free to open up in a very vulnerable way.

Most IMers and MySpacers report feeling freer to self-disclose personal feelings and thoughts to someone online than they would face-to-face. And, let's face it: online can feel much safer. Something about the online environment makes opening up easier and less risky. Instead of looking into someone's disinterested or judgmental eyes, teenage computer users can type into the warm and forgiving computer. They can think about what they are going to say—crafting every word to make it sound just right. They don't have to worry about the little smirks or sideways glances that can communicate shame or failure to a teenager. Instead, they have control of their environment. The timing, the language, even the responses seem much more manageable—especially when it is so easy to read closeness into the conversation and the relationship.

These attributes of online communication combine with the private context many users experience as they type alone and late at night to create a powerful feeling of intimacy. One high school student likened an IM conversation to writing in a journal. That is a powerful statement. On one hand, the technology is meeting a need many teenagers have to work through complex emotions and thoughts. On the other hand, the technology seems to encourage teens to confuse a one-way "spilling your guts" with genuine relationship building.

Unfortunately, one of the very real consequences of heavy online use is that teens begin to develop a distorted view of what it means to be a friend. It becomes more about talking and less about listening, more about telling and less about sharing, more about taking and less about giving.

MAKE A CONNECTION: **Ask if your teen feels that it is easier to open up online than in person. Then ask why. Your child may never have thought about how the technology changes the way he or she communicates. If your teen is older, it may be interesting to begin a discussion about how this pull toward online self-disclosure changes his or her relationships.**

Distorting Friendships

How we view friendships says a lot about what is important to us. Jesus provides a powerful example of a relationship that is built, not on taking, but on giving. He came to earth to spend some quality face-to face time with his creation, listening, teaching, guiding, and ultimately sacrificing everything. Scripture is filled with examples of how Jesus cared for and ministered to those he met, whether a Samaritan woman, a tax collector, or a betrayer. A stark contrast emerges between this kind of loving, compassionate intimacy and that created on a computer screen between two individuals who may be more concerned with "self-messaging" than self-sacrifice. Online communication technology can create a false sense of intimacy that has the potential to redefine the moral basis of teenage friendship.

In addition to failing to comprehend the giving nature of friendships, it is also possible that by building and maintaining friendships in this very stark, fast-paced, self-based medium, young people are losing many of the relational skills necessary for getting along with people. According to George Barna, "Relationships are more highly esteemed by today's teens than baby boomers when they were the same age. Yet, while many teens desire deeper, lasting relationships, they do not have the communication skills, the commitment to loyalty and forgiveness, and the emotional maturity to foster such binding."[1] Unfortunately, using the computer to enhance friendships may be making this problem even more serious as teens learn to multitask their friendships, surfing in and out of conversations, conflicts, and commitments.

The absence of real-live interpersonal contact can also distort a teen's understanding of other people. According to communication scholar Michael Bugeja, "People deprived of interpersonal contact eventually suspect rather than trust others because their perception of reality has been skewed, prompting misinterpretation of messages and motives, thereby harming relationships."[2] Instead of developing patience and longsuffering to figure out how to get along with people, technology encourages teens to disengage from things that are not fun or helpful, easily clicking to another screen or another friend who has more to offer.

Overall, online communication technology has had a slow but insidious effect on how our kids understand their relationships and work through their friendships. Fantasy and wishful thinking can easily fill in the blanks left by the lack of nonverbal communication. That leaves a clear gap between what is happening in the real world and what seems to be going on in the virtual world. The lack of real-life interactions can also limit the development of certain relational skills, such as empathy, commitment, forgiveness, and even the simple ability to read someone's body language to find out what he or she really means. As wise parents, we need to keep a steady eye on our children's relational health and friendship skills.

MAKE A CONNECTION: **Watch for signs of faltering relational skills in your teen. Every teen struggles with learning how to be a friend, but things like lack of commitment, selfishness, and an inability to work through tough relational issues may be related to heavy use of online communication technology. Before pulling the plug, however, ask if your teen thinks IM and MySpace have impacted how patient he or she is with friends and how well he or she is willing or able to really listen to those friends.**

Recreating Community, Remitting Responsibility

Clearly, social networking technology impacts how teens build and maintain friendships. The Internet has also changed the way many young people understand and participate in "community." According to sociologists, communities are important social structures that help young people see how adults are supposed to act.

The Place of Community

Think back about the role your community played in your growing-up experience. I couldn't get away with much when I was growing up. The women in the church kept a sharp eye on all the kids—from the toddlers to the high schoolers. They taught us not to run in the halls, and they showed us how to fold our hands and pray. They taught us how to let loose and fill the room with laughter, and they showed us how to support one another with meals, cards, and prayers. Those women, though probably not the kind of people I would choose to IM or blog, played a vital role in helping me understand what it meant to live as a Christian and what it meant to be part of a community of believers.

My neighborhood community also taught me about how other people lived. One family down the road had a dad who smoked and drank too much. While I learned how those behaviors impacted the family, I also learned that those kids were every bit as loving and vital as my church friends who came from much more perfect-looking families. Another family up the hill had a daughter who was a bit overweight and not very "cool." She taught me what it meant to have compassion and how hurtful it was to be written off by people who never took time to listen or find the value. My neighborhood community taught me about diversity and how to live in a world full of multiple perspectives. It taught me the value of people who were like me and the value of those who were very different. It taught me how to cherish those who had a lot to give and those who had little to give. Would I have chosen to IM these people with whom I couldn't initially relate? Probably not.

My community also helped me define who I was. As a teenager, I remember trying to figure out how I could be like everyone else at the same time I was unique. Along with wearing bell-bottoms, platform shoes, and watermelon lip gloss, I discovered I was good at public speaking, playing the bass clarinet, and making people laugh. Unfortunately, the bass clarinet thing never really panned out, but the feedback I received from friends, teachers, and adults who were significant to me helped refine my understanding of how I was uniquely and wonderfully made. Looking back, I see that I was blessed with a feeling of belongingness that came from a stable and supportive community. Those relationships with kids, teenagers, and adults helped me understand how to act, how to see things from multiple perspectives, and how to use my unique qualities to support and strengthen this ongoing social system called community.

The New Place of Community

As essential as the role of community is to the development of young people, the way it plays out in the lives of today's teens is changing faster than most people realize. In the "good ol' days," our community was made up of people in the neighborhood. News was shared over the picket fence (or at least that's what it looked like in the movies). We lived and worked with the same families for most of our growing-up years. When Mr. Rogers called us a good neighbor, we knew what it meant.

Today's young people, however, have a very different understanding of neighborhoods. Instead of Mr. McFeely stopping by to say hi or the corner storeowner knowing our names and our usual order, our neighborhoods are often filled with full-time working parents who get home just in time to run the kids to the next structured event. We live in a much more mobile society with new people moving in and out of neighborhoods, often with very different backgrounds or family experiences.

While these changes do not necessarily mean that we can't connect with each other, it does mean that many of our "communities" or places where we find belongingness are no longer based in a place traditionally called a neighborhood. For instance, my family tends to be much closer to our church friends, school friends, and work friends than to the new neighbors we wave at as we drive by to get to our next event. The idea and place of community has changed for all of us. This change, however, has been especially noticeable in how high-tech teens find and experience community.

MAKE A CONNECTION: **Ask where your teen thinks his or her "community" is. Who is helping your child develop into a young adult who knows the difference between right and wrong? Where does your teen meet older people who can teach lessons based on a wealth of experience? Who has helped your child understand his or her talents and special gifts? What draws these people together?**

Challenges of the New Community

As teens take after their parents and lead busier, more potentially superficial and fragmented lives, it is no surprise that they turn to technology to help them meet so many of their developmental needs. Online teens often substitute the powerful diversity of multi-generational, traditional, place-based communities with virtually-based and often unrelated groups of barely committed friends. This process of revaluing and replacing traditional community affects young people in many ways, including challenges related to responsibility, diversity, and fragmentation.

Responsibility. As children grow into well-functioning adults, a key change is the development of a sense of right and wrong. That's where community comes in. A true community teaches teens about boundaries. Whether it be a mother, a friend's mother, a grandparent, or a neighbor, members of a community teach kids what is acceptable and what is not in a way that bears out a commitment to the ultimate growth and well-being of the child. As a result, teens see and expect certain consequences for hurting others and behaving in destructive ways.

So what happens when no adults are around? What happens when teens know that most adults are too confused or over-whelmed to figure out what is going on in the virtual world? What happens when the real-life consequences of bad behavior are hidden by stark text and miles of Internet wiring? You can guess what happens: very bad behavior.

Kids do things online that they would never do in real life. Communication scholars call this the online disinhibition effect. Kids call it lying, swearing, bullying, gossiping, sex-talk, and just plain meanness. I have spoken with many concerned parents who decided to read some of their kids' instant messages or found and read their teen's MySpace page. They describe the experience with pain in their voices, wondering how such filth could come from the children they have always seen as being sweet and kind. Unfortunately, something about the online environment frees kids to act in less than appropriate ways.

I asked teens, "Why is it so easy to act badly online?" They came up with some very insightful answers. First, they attribute some of the negative behavior to the fact that there is no adult supervision. Kids figure they won't get caught and won't get in trouble, so they push the boundaries. And that makes sense—to a certain degree. Adult supervision will control certain behaviors, but when it comes down to it, peers often have more control over kids than adults. It would seem that, for some reason, peers do not have the same "rules" for online conduct as they do for "real life." Something about being online makes it socially okay among kids to behave in ways that would be considered inappropriate in face-to-face contexts. Lack of adult supervision may be a real problem, but something more is going on.

A second reason teens gave for why it's "not that big of a deal" if kids act badly online is that "it just doesn't seem as real." When kids are mean or raunchy, their behavior isn't taken as seriously as it would be in real life because it isn't as "real." It is easier to feel okay about lying or pushing someone around because, after all, "it isn't real." According to many young people, doing things online simply isn't the same as doing things in real life.

That led to my next question: If hurtful behaviors aren't as "real" online, do they still hurt? There was a bit more debate on this question, but the final consensus was that it didn't hurt as bad because it was easier to "blow it off" or "just turn off the computer." Somehow, young people justify much of their bad behavior by making a distinction between the real and the virtual worlds. Unfortunately, as much as teens try and convince us and themselves that the real and the virtual are quite separate, there is no doubt that these worlds intersect in ways that make virtual words every bit as real, hurtful, and damaging as something said face-to-face.

A third reason middle schoolers gave for why it is easier to be mean online is that "you don't have to see the hurt in their eyes." In other words, the real-life consequences of hurtful behavior are virtually removed from online interactions. Simone can feel powerful and cut someone down. But unlike a face-to-face confrontation, she doesn't have to come face-to-face with the interpersonal fallout. She doesn't have to look into the eyes of the person she just hurt. She can get in and out, relishing the rush of power she feels in establishing dominance over another. As a result, the whole thing doesn't seem quite as real. She has all the fun of being a powerful bully with very few of consequences.

The next question that comes to mind for IMers is "If kids are behaving so badly online, why don't you just tell an adult?"

According to the teens I interviewed, the answer is clear: since it isn't "real" swearing or "real" bullying or "real" gossip or "real" sex, it's not that big of a deal. And it certainly doesn't make sense to drag an adult into an adolescent world. Ratting on someone in the real world for something he or she did in a virtual world just doesn't seem to jive for many kids.

MediaWise.com provides an additional thought as to why most kids are reluctant to turn in their peers who behave badly online: they are afraid their parents will overreact and take away their computer in an effort to "protect" them. Faced with the alternatives of losing computer privileges or putting up with a bully, a gossip, or a meanie who is throwing virtual stones, most kids stick with sucking up and shutting up. So where does that leave us? Out of our desire to protect our kids, we may *over*react and scare them away or we may *under*react and leave them with virtual scars that hurt every bit as real ones.

MAKE A CONNECTION: **Ask your teens the same questions: Why are kids meaner online? Does it hurt as badly when people are mean online as when they are mean face-to-face? Are kids less apt to tell on someone who did something wrong online? Why? These questions can lead to some interesting conversations–as long as you try your hardest not to overreact to your child's answers.**

Diversity. When kids replace a real-life community with a virtual group of friends, the lack of responsibility to each other is evident as kids do things to tear each other down. Another consequence of the high-tech approach to community is the way kids are able to pick and choose whom they hang out with and whom they choose to avoid. The clear result is a lack of diversity in their lives. Think about when you have learned some of your greatest life lessons. Those times were probably when you stretched yourself to move out of your comfort zone—to move beyond what was normal and expected. Maybe someone challenged your thinking to see things in ways you had never thought of before. Maybe you went on a mission trip or spent time at a homeless shelter or chose to hang around someone who made you uncomfortable.

Maybe you worked through a conflict with a friend or family member, learning how to live with someone who sees things from a different perspective.

Christian community is all about diversity. Unfortunately, when young people situate their social life online, they miss out on experiences that would stretch them and expand their minds and remind them of how big God truly is. They tend to retain a fairly unsophisticated view of how people work and are less able to see things from another person's perspective, making conflicts more difficult to manage and relationships harder to maintain. Vital relational skills like empathy and flexibility may be overtaken with a myopic, self-centered rigidity that makes negotiation, compromise, and understanding much more difficult to achieve. Heavy online users may grow up seeing God and his big, beautiful world in very limited and immature ways.

MAKE A CONNECTION: **Talk about a time when your child learned something new by going out of his or her comfort zone–a time when he or she was really stretched. Then ask if your teen thinks some of those kinds of experiences might be missed in a virtual world. Why or why not?**

Fragmentation. The other day a dad pulled me aside. He was frazzled and frustrated because he had just found his daughter's MySpace site. His beautiful little girl, who he knew in his heart was good and kind, had a site full of bad attitude and porn. She talked about sex like she was experienced. She used language that would embarrass a honky-tonk bartender, and she said incredibly nasty things on her blog about some girls from school she had played with since she was little. He was heartbroken. Probably the most difficult thing was that, in the background section of her MySpace profile, she had checked the box identifying herself as a Christian.

Unfortunately, such scenarios are not uncommon. Way too often I meet a student from school or church who seems like a fine Christian young person. Joe Christian is well mannered and clean-cut, he can quote Scripture, and he is even kind to children. Then I go on his MySpace site. The identity he is portraying to his virtual friends is disturbingly different from what he portrays on Sunday mornings. Now, most kids are going to behave differently in front of their parents and other adults than they do with their friends. The real trouble, however, according to many of the youth pastors I talk with, is that kids don't see the problem. They don't see a contradiction in being a Christian in one setting and a wild kid who is living on the edge in another setting. To make matters worse, technology like MySpace clearly encourages lying, exaggeration, and even complete fabrication. Kids routinely experiment with who they want to be by putting things on their profiles that are more about who they wish they were instead of who they actually are.

It is easy for kids to conclude that these exaggerations are not that big of a deal because what they are doing "isn't real," but at the same time, a disconcerting fragmentation is taking place in these young persons' identities. Things like wholeness and integrity are replaced with superficiality and compartmentalization. It is difficult for kids to maintain a sense of self—rooted and grounded in who God wants them to be—when the schism between the real and the virtual becomes shaded with complexity and overlap. When young people are surrounded, supported, and enveloped by a real live community, it is much more difficult for them to experience fragmentation between contexts. Community calls young people toward consistency and integrity. It is essential that we help move our kids toward relationships that will help them understand what it means to be a follower of Christ in *every* context—whether real or virtual.

MAKE A CONNECTION: **Ask if your child sees kids who are completely different in an online context than they are face-to-face. Ask your teen why he or she thinks that happens.**

As we have seen, online communication technology can have a significant impact on a teenager's experience of community. When teenagers can flit from one community to the next with few commitments and even less willingness to engage in unpleasant learning experiences, they no longer learn the lessons that help them become mature Christian adults. This "networked individualism" can create teenagers who struggle to maintain a holistic understanding of who they are and what it means to be a person of integrity in a very complex high-tech world.[3]

Fragmenting Faith, Following an Online God

Living in a world that blurs the distinction between real and virtual has critical implications for how our kids understand who God is and how he expects them to act. One of the ways that God helps us understand his character and his vision for our lives is through our relationships with others and our commitment to a Christian community. It is through other people that we learn things like self-sacrifice and unconditional love. It is through Christian community that we learn what it means to be committed to the well-being of others, becoming part of something bigger and more significant than ourselves. When young people begin to experience distorted versions of friendship and community, their understanding of an almighty God also becomes distorted. Three areas of concern can be connected with these changes, including online users' tendency toward compartmentalization, separation from creation, and search for true connection.

Compartmentalization

One of the challenges faced by Christians in our postmodern, high-tech culture is the pull toward superficiality and fragmentation. Our lives are often consumed by a lot of unrelated, insignificant things. The same is true for the lives of busy teenagers. Moreover, technology allows them to have numerous superficial relationships. Deep-running connections and commitments that help make life meaningful and purposeful may be absent from the lives of our teenagers.

According to communication scholar Quentin Schultz, "One of our most fundamental choices in the information age is whether to approach life superficially as tourists or more intimately as sojourners."[4] When we consider how high-tech-teens' view of God may be impacted by the technology they cling to, it may be helpful to compare the tourist's view of a "nice to know but fairly irrelevant" God to the sojourner's view of the "almighty, deeply relevant" God. The tourist can easily come and go, accessing God's promises much like using an ATM. An understanding of God's power may be limited to specific situations, becoming nothing more than a compartmentalized, use as you need, dismiss as you must spiritual approach to life. The sojourner on the other hand takes time and energy to stop and think. By meditating on Scripture and on God's creation, the sojourner is able to see the intricate connections that run throughout life. God's mighty hand is seen in everything. This understanding brings the sojourner to a humble and awe-inspired view of who God is as well as to a natural desire for worship and obedience.

One of the very real challenges for all of us in this postmodern culture is to be sojourners seeking truth and righteousness in a patient and significant way. This is especially difficult for teenagers who see much of life through a computer screen. One of the most influential things we parents can do is to help our children cultivate a grand and awe-inspiring view of God—one that envelops every part of their lives—whether in the real or the virtual world. By reminding them in word and deed that Christ has something to say about every relationship, every situation, every feeling, and every instant message, we can help enrich and enlarge their views of God. By encouraging them to take time to think and to meditate—to slow down long enough to let their minds focus on what is important—we can help them understand how deeply fulfilling the Christian life can be.

There is one catch to this approach, however. We have to be willing to do the same thing—to disengage from our busy schedules long enough to reconnect with what is important. We have to figure out how a relevant God can be part of every area of our lives—not just our time at church or a quick quiet time as we rush out the door for work. Without a doubt, the best way for our kids to understand how God can play a part in their high-tech lives is for us to role model how God plays a part in our hectic, everyday lives. It would be easier if we could just give our kids a book or have them watch a video, but this kind of teaching takes more from us. It takes a commitment to become sojourners who contemplatively and humbly seek after the truth and wisdom God has promised us. It is only then that our kids will be motivated to slow down and experience the true fulfillment that comes with honoring and worshiping the almighty God.

PARENT TIP: **Take time to disconnect from your busy schedule and reconnect with the true giver of life. Figure out how you can take time to slow down—and don't forget to let your kids in on what you learn.**

Separation from Creation

A second clear challenge that arises in how high-tech teens view God and relate to him can be seen in how they relate to the creation all around them. Certainly one of the drawbacks of heavy online use is how it disconnects kids, not only from reality, but also from nature. I won't even get into how our kids are less active, more out of shape, and more prone to common diseases of a sedentary society—mostly because it hits a little close to home. However guilty I may feel about not rushing outside to play with my children, I must acknowledge this equation: more media time inside equals less unconnected time outside. Consider for a minute what kind of impact this disconnection with the outdoors may have on a teenager's ability to comprehend the bigness and creativity of God.

Nature influences how we understand and relate to God. Think about a time when nature took your breath away. Maybe it was the view from the top of a mountain or the moon sparkling over a calm ocean or the glistening sun on fresh-fallen snow. Now think about the impact if, instead of seeing it in real life—of smelling it and feeling it and breathing it—you saw a picture of it. Even if it's a good picture, it's really not the same. A picture doesn't have the power to convey the same sense of awe, majesty, and God's creativity. The picture can be held in our hands, but the actual creation holds us as part of an interconnected system of order and splendor. When young people spend a lot of time in front of a computer screen, much of life becomes reduced to snapshots.

They may look real, but they're not. When we lose connection with nature, we lose connection with our Creator.

Every time my family goes to camp, I am amazed with the things I see—not in the trees or the lake or even the cute little woodland creatures. I am amazed at the change I see in my children. It takes a day or two, but eventually they disconnect from the artificial light and the superficial IM conversations. They run around, they swim, they sit and talk with their friends. And when the sun sets over the lake, they come together at the top of the hill and marvel at God's handiwork. God makes his power and majesty known no more clearly than through his creation. And whether it be taking in big snowy mountain views or watching a little ant haul away a crumb, we find that nature is full of lessons. When we help our kids reconnect with nature, we help them reconnect with a fuller view of who God is and a better understanding of how they fit in.

Search for the True Connection

The final challenge of maintaining an accurate view of God in a postmodern world can be seen in how desperately our kids long for true connection. Throughout this book, I have talked about using the computer to find "connections." While these connections can feel very real at times, there is simply no replacement for the touch of a friend or the hug of a parent. According to seminary professor and author John Jewell, "Virtual community does not have 'real presence.' For Christian people, the incarnation is fundamental to who we are as persons and who we are as a community."[5] Christ came to earth in the form of a man—not a profile or a blog or an instant message. God designed humans to connect with one another in real life, real time, and real space. Sharing the here and now is fundamentally different than connecting through words on a computer screen in a virtual time and a virtual space.

And as essential as it is for young people to learn how to act in the here and now, making real-life, heartfelt connections, it is even more important for them to find the ultimate source of connection. One reason adolescents so desperately turn to the computer is because they are having trouble finding something in their lives that makes them feel full, purposeful, and loved. That something is a personal relationship with Jesus Christ. Ultimately, all the MySpace friends and IM buddies in the world will never equal the joy that comes with being a disciple of Christ.

So what does that mean for parents? Never fear. Whether in a quiet place in their room or on a MySpace blog on their computer, Christ is knocking on the door of the hearts of our young people. If they choose to open the door and invite him in, he will not forsake them. Jesus is with them in the safety of our homes where we can watch everything they do, as well as with them when they are spending time with friends on the Internet away from our control. Once they make the ultimate connection, young people will find that many of the needs they look to the computer to meet will seem less important. And while we can do everything humanly possible to hold our kids tightly, protecting them from the evils of this world, we ultimately have to release our grip and let God take them and mold them in ways we can't even imagine.

Social networking sites and instant messaging have a lot of potential and a lot of pitfalls. By better understanding what the challenges are and how technology can change the way our kids think, we can help them use technology in healthy and productive ways. We need to keep talking with our kids, encouraging them to use online communication technology with their eyes wide open to the ways it can impact their views of reality, friendships, community, and faith.

"The Bad" Discussion Starters

Relationships

Talk about times your teen has had misunderstandings online.

Challenge teens who are seriously dating to spend less time online and more time face-to-face.

Be aware of faltering relationship skills in your teen: impatience, inability to read or effectively use nonverbal cues, lack of empathy, inability to listen, etc.

Community

Talk with your teen about which adults have impacted him or her most in life.

Ask what "community" means to your teen. How is community experienced online?

Ask if your teen thinks it is easier to be mean online. Why?

Ask about a time your teen really stepped out of his or her comfort zone. Talk about how living life in a virtual world might limit that kind of experience.

Faith

Share with your child things that God has been teaching you.

Talk about how a high-tech life can make it harder for people to connect with God.

CHAPTER 5

Fearless parenting
"But My Kids Know So Much More Than I Do!"

Being a parent is tough. It's tough when we are bombarded with stories of young girls and boys being stalked by very bad people who use MySpace and instant messaging to track their prey. It's tough when our kids implore, finagle, and ceaselessly plead with us to let them use the latest and greatest technology because everyone else does. It's tough when we just don't have the time or energy to figure out how all this technology works. But, as tough as being a parent is, we are still the parents. It is still up to us to protect our kids. We are still the ones who are commissioned by God to teach our kids about how they are supposed to act—both in the real and the virtual worlds.

So how do we do that in a way that makes sense for our families? This final chapter offers some very specific ideas about how to approach the challenging task of parenting an instant messaging, MySpace-loving teen. The first section deals with some of the very scary things that can happen to kids and how you can keep yours safe. The second section deals with proactive, everyday things that can both protect kids and empower them to be wise users of technology.

When Friends Become Strangers and
Strangers Become Friends

As I sat and listened to my friend tell me the story of his daughter, Sadie, my heart broke. MySpace was the portal through which evil had entered his home and deeply hurt his teenage daughter. It happened about a year ago. They noticed their once bubbly, sweet daughter began to change. She seemed moody and quick to start a fight. Her grades dropped and she hardly left the house. She started spending less time with her friends. One day one of those friends called in a panic. She didn't know what else to do because she was afraid Sadie was going to hurt herself. The friend told Sadie's parents of their daughter's MySpace site and the posting she had just read that talked about suicide. The dad thanked the friend, hung up the phone, and logged on to the computer. He couldn't believe it. It was Sadie's site, but nothing about it resembled his daughter. The picture, instead of showing a slightly overweight young girl struggling with acne, revealed a beautiful young blond woman who looked like she was ready for some seductive activity. Other pictures featured pornographic poses and involved guys he had never met. Sadie had blogs that explicitly talked about sex and the kinds of things she liked to do.

Heartbroken, the parents knocked on Sadie's door. After some talking, screaming, and crying, Sadie finally told them what was going on. While on MySpace, she had met a guy from school—or at least he said he was from school. He had sent her a message, and when she went on his site, he had a lot of the same friends she did, so she figured it was okay to get to know him better. As they talked, he made her feel special and pretty—something no guy had ever done before. They set up a time to meet at the local mall. When she got there, he was with some of his other friends. They all just hung out together—no big deal. They continued to correspond over IM and MySpace, and it wasn't long before the guy began asking her to talk to him about sex. It was awkward at first; she didn't know what to say. He helped her describe things to him, all the while telling her how beautiful she was and how much he loved her. He eventually persuaded her to post pictures of herself on her MySpace page. He told her what to do and praised her when she posted the images.

Eventually Sadie agreed to meet the guy again. Because she felt as if they had developed a very intimate relationship, she went to his apartment. When she arrived she found her "boyfriend" along with more of his friends. After talking for a while, things began to get out of hand. Pretty soon the guys were raping her as her boyfriend watched. It was hours before Sadie could get out. She stumbled home, ashamed and devastated. She didn't feel she could tell her parents because they hadn't wanted her to have a MySpace site in the first place. She knew she had messed up and was utterly humiliated. She didn't know where to turn, so she went on MySpace and bared her soul in her virtual world.

Sadie had been the victim of a sexual predator. He had found Sadie on MySpace and had keyed in on the vulnerable things she had put on her site. He found her school, her friends, even her interests online, then put them into his profile. He lied about his age and where he went to school. What is most significant, he knew how MySpace and IM heightened feelings of intimacy and took advantage of that knowledge. He was able to make Sadie believe he cared about her and could be trusted.

I share this story not to scare parents, but to make a point: very real danger is associated with online communication technology. Part of the danger comes about when kids start building relationships with strangers—people they have never met face-to-face. Part of it comes when they start down the slippery slope of talking about sex over the Internet—something they would never do in a face-to-face environment. Both of these challenges require the diligence and wisdom of involved parents.

Stranger Danger

Identifying strangers. There are a few things we as parents can do to protect and train our kids. The first thing has to do with meeting strangers. When my kids were young, I did quite a good job of training them to identify strangers. We role-played what they should do if a scary man drove up in a rusty van and asked them if they wanted candy. We took turns screaming, "Leave me alone!"

and running around the front yard. My kids knew how to kick and run. Unfortunately, it wasn't until recently that I talked to my teenagers about how to identify online strangers. Online strangers look a lot less strange. In fact, they may look pretty nice. They may say nice things, and they may seem to have a mutual network of friends. They may actually seem to be a lot nicer than most of the people a teenager hangs out with in real life since so much of the relationship is produced by conveniently "filling in the blanks." Honestly, it is hard to teach a kid to scream, kick, and run when he or she is feeling so intimate with a person their parents have identified as a "stranger."

So what is a parent to do? The first step is to come to an understanding with your child about who should be labeled a stranger. Anyone your child has not met face-to-face is someone who falls into the same category as the guy who drives up in a rusty van and offers candy to small children. It doesn't matter if the person is a friend of a friend or if he knows all the same people as your child or if he shares interests with your child and they get along really well. Until your child has evidence that the person is not dangerous, he or she should approach online communication with that person with an optimum amount of skepticism and distrust. That is a fundamental lesson we need to teach our kids from the minute they log on.

Avoiding strangers. The easiest way to protect online teens from strangers who want to do them harm is to help them figure out how to avoid strangers altogether. There are a few ways to do that. Let's start with MySpace. Lots of kids like MySpace because they can meet "new people" (in my book, that's just a fancy term for strangers). If kids choose a strict privacy setting for their profile, it limits how much social networking they can do. If kids do not choose to have a privacy setting, they open up their information for everyone to see. That leaves you with a dilemma: how do you balance what your child wants with what may be safest? It is a dilemma you will need to work out based on your child and your relationship. If your child is using or is considering using MySpace, it makes sense to sit down with him or her and come to a mutual agreement about MySpace privacy settings.

Once you have the whole privacy thing figured out, however, don't stop there; it is quite easy to get around a MySpace privacy setting. As mentioned earlier, the most common problem with limited access is that kids will let anyone be their "friend." Unfortunately, that defeats the purpose of a privacy setting. After you and your child agree on a MySpace privacy setting, you should also agree on what constitutes a "friend." Some parents negotiate a policy stating that no "friends" will be accepted if they haven't been met face-to-face. Some parents agree to let their kids use MySpace if their kids, in turn, agree to use MySpace only to network with their face-to-face friends, forgoing the opportunity to make new friends online. These kinds of restrictions may work better for newer MySpace users, serving as a stepping-stone to more open access.

While it is easy to imagine stalkers using MySpace, instant messaging should make all of us do a little shaking in our shoes. Keep in mind, most kids use IM exclusively for talking with their real-life friends. When the occasional stranger does pop up, however, our children can get into dangerous territory. Because IM creates such an intimate environment, strangers can quickly take advantage of a young person's usually skeptical eye. I would strongly advise you to talk to your kids about IMing people they don't know. It is not a good idea. Period. And it doesn't take much to train a teenager to react immediately to an IM coming from someone he or she doesn't know. Many of the kids I have talked with definitely know how to block strange IMs or how to tell someone they don't know to "get lost." A little parent-to-teen talk, a little story, a little persuasion, and you can quickly teach your teen to tell off a strange IMer just as clearly and forcefully as he or she was trained in kindergarten to kick and run if a stranger offered candy. It doesn't take much—but make sure you don't assume your kids already know what to do.

Content Danger

Identifying and keeping out strangers is without doubt a vital first step in protecting our kids. But what about other dangers? We also need to teach our kids about watching what they say.

The myth of privacy. As sophisticated as they like to act, our kids can still be naïve. They can hear it from us, from the newspapers, and from stories on the TV news, but when they are online, enveloped in their personal virtual world, it is hard to remember that there are some things that should always be kept private. Unfortunately, teenage MySpacers make it all too easy for people to find them, rarely thinking twice about putting things like their full name, cell phone, address, and school name online for anyone to see.

In addition to putting *too much* personal information on MySpace, many students never consider the consequences of putting the *wrong kind* of information on MySpace. For instance, a sexy shirt and suggestive pose may get some of the guys at school all excited, but it may also catch the eye of someone who is looking for a lot more than a little conversation. Big talk about drugs, sex, partying, and self-destructive behavior may be exaggerated or even made up to look cool, but it may also catch the eye of someone looking for a teen who is in trouble and easy to manipulate. Wild pictures and lewd conversations may feel fun and edgy to post online, but a teen may learn the hard way that potential employers who regularly check MySpace for background information on applicants don't find it quite so funny. The bottom line is that MySpace is not private. Even with privacy settings, a lot of people see teenagers' MySpace sites. And just because they delete things doesn't mean they're gone. Raunchy pictures can be downloaded and widely shared, haunting a teen for the rest of his or her life. We need to have regular conversations with our kids about the kinds of things they are putting "out there" for all of their "friends" to see.

MySpace isn't the only place where privacy is a convenient misperception. Private IM conversations can also become quite public. While these conversations may not be as accessible to strangers, they can easily end up being read by people for whom they were not originally intended. Unfortunately, it is not uncommon for young IMers to cut and paste conversations, forwarding personal interactions to a lot of friends. In this way, a small, hurtful trick can turn into a big mess. Suddenly numerous friends see things they shouldn't, making the social fallout swift and severe.

Moreover, plenty of deception occurs through instant messaging. Someone may be baring their soul to a friend, only to find out it is the little brother who is on the other end of the computer. Once again, private information isn't quite as private as most users assume. It makes sense to talk with kids about the myth of privacy on IM, urging them to avoid sending things that are too personal. Being discreet may keep them from getting hurt or hurting someone else.

The slippery slope of cybersex. Another real danger of instant messaging is how easily communication can turn intimate. Two young people can start off talking about regular, everyday things and end up getting into a sexual relationship that can be even more confusing, hurtful, and addictive than one in real life. The slippery slope is easy. The myth that says "It's not real, so it's okay" helps get kids started. Pretty soon they are talking about things that would be way too embarrassing to discuss in real life. As they slide on down the slope, discussions about sex become more intense and compelling. Pretty soon conversations describing detailed acts of sex become an intimate, hidden part of the relationship. Unfortunately, once a relationship ends, the emotional scars can be every bit as real as if the sex happened in the backseat of the family van. There is also a natural progression from IM sex to online pornography, which is every bit as accessible by teens as the TV listings or Sunday newspaper. And don't think it won't happen to your kid because he or she knows better. It can happen to every kind of kid.

We must not be naïve about the possibility of our kids stepping on the slippery slope. They are at a time in their lives when they are open to experimentation. The computer offers easy access and a convenient virtual rationalization. That means parents have to be alert. We need to have our eyes, our ears, and even our hearts open. Keeping our eyes open to changes in our children may help us catch a problem before it goes too far. Maybe they spend a lot more private or late-night time on the computer; maybe they are more withdrawn and moody; maybe they have a new romantic relationship that seems to have taken off overnight or a relationship that they will no longer talk with you about; maybe they seem to be disconnecting from their real-life friends. Keeping our ears open to conversations they may have can also help us intervene. They may drop hints about things happening online. And keeping our hearts open will help us better understand our kids when they get into trouble. We need to be able to connect with our kids—even on topics as uncomfortable as cybersex. As difficult as they may be, open discussions are imperative. We need to let our kids know how easy it is to get sucked into an online sexual relationship. And we need to be able to ask questions and listen to them talk about what is real and what they see as virtual fun.

By talking about the temptations of online sexual conversations *before* the temptation comes up, we can better equip our kids to see the real-life consequences of seemingly unreal but quite intoxicating online behavior. By keeping a dialogue open with our kids who are in "serious" dating relationships, we can help them fight sexual temptations that have stealthily moved from the family room couch to the family room computer.

Bully Danger

Protecting teenagers from harm is no small task. Having discussions about online strangers, privacy, and cybersex is certainly a first step. Unfortunately, there are lots of everyday social dangers waiting to befall teenagers who are very concerned about how they fit in. The computer can take difficult adolescent drama, such as gossiping, cattiness, or even outright bullying, and turbocharge those behaviors. A fight between two friends can hit the Internet and suddenly involve an entire social group. On a quick trip to MySpace, kids can post embarrassing pictures and cruel jokes, stories, or drawings in public spheres. A simple shared password that ends up in the wrong hands might result in deceptive messages being sent from someone's IM account. Power-starved teens can coerce and even threaten kids online, making those kids feel powerless, trapped, isolated, and scared to log on. According to MediaWise.org, 53 percent of online kids admitted to saying something mean online and 42 percent of online kids have been bullied over the computer. To make matters worse, kids are reluctant to tell a parent about things that happen online. Fifty-eight percent of online kids have decided not to tell an adult about something hurtful that happened to them online.

What is a parent to do? The first discussion you may want to have with your teens has to do with values. Being mean to someone online is the same as being mean to someone's face. You want to make sure your kids carry the same values learned at home and at church with them when they travel online. After all, you don't want them using the computer as an excuse to get back at someone or using MySpace or instant messaging to hurt someone else. One of the best words of advice for online kids is never to send or post a message when angry. Instead of immediately responding to something that makes them boil, teach your kids to let things cool down first. Encourage them to deal with conflict offline—they will have fewer misunderstandings, and situations won't spiral out of control quite so quickly.

Second, advise your teens not to share their online passwords with anyone. Even though sharing passwords is a new symbol of true friendship, those passwords can easily be used against a young person. Make sure your children understand the negative potential of letting someone else have access to their online identity.

Finally, let your teens know that it is okay to come to you if something happens. Let them know you won't blame them or take away their computer privileges if someone else hurts them or scares them or threatens them in some way. Remind your kids that you are there to help them with things that stem from real life *and* from online life. Threats or bullying cannot be tolerated on the school bus or on the computer. That means we need to convince our kids to take online hurtful behavior seriously enough to take action.

Some very bad things can happen to our kids when they venture online. By training children to know how to act online and how to protect themselves, we can empower them to use communication technology in wise and purposeful ways.

The Fine Balance between Trusting and Protecting

At this point, I hope you have been encouraged to talk with your kids. There are a lot of places to start, and you will most likely find that your teenagers appreciate your interest. A more practical issue still remains, however. How do we proactively manage this technology that has taken such a prevalent spot in our homes? The solution lies in an ongoing *process* rather than a static list of things to do. As kids change and mature, as we grow more confident and knowledgeable, and as technology changes at breakneck speed, we continually need to be talking with our kids, setting guidelines, monitoring their behavior, and finding nontechnological ways for them to socialize. By walking through the following four steps with your teenager, you should be able to determine together what is best for your teenager and your family.

Step 1: Talk

As I have spoken with parent groups, I am consistently asked about disciplinary steps parents should take to limit their kids' use of technology. I am asked about spy software, about blocking software, and about different ways to catch kids messing up. While these things can certainly play a part in how we help our kids use technology wisely, the place to start is by sitting down and having a conversation. Let's face it: for the most part, we really don't know how our kids use online communication technology. We see them sitting at the computer or text messaging on their cell phones, but we probably don't know why they use it or how much it means to them. So before we start thinking of ways to limit them or trap them, let's spend some time thinking of ways to understand and encourage them.

There are many ways to start a discussion. If your teens use online communication technology, ask why they like it and how they use it on a typical day. Ask how they think it has impacted them and their friendships. If your children don't use the technology but are pleading with you to let them start, ask them what they hope to gain by being online. Ask why their friends like it and what problems those friends have had with it. Ask your kids to think about ways the technology might impact them—both good and bad. By using open-ended questions at the beginning of conversations, we can get our kids talking. One thing I have consistently found to be the case: when given a little opening, kids love talking about their technology. They love teaching adults about the wonders of this new form of relationship building. They even seem to like thinking about the wider impact of how technology might be changing them. If you haven't tried it yet, start by asking your kids what they think. You may be amazed to find out what is going on in your teenagers' high-tech minds.

Step 2: Set Guidelines

Once you have begun a conversation about the positive and negative aspects of using MySpace and instant messaging, it is much easier to come to an agreement about guidelines. The most effective guidelines will be those that are negotiated and developed together. Following are some things to take into consideration when developing guidelines.

Time limits. Through surveys and interviews and in focus groups and discussions I have had with parents, kids, and youth pastors, the most consistent message I have received is that kids need limits. College students, especially, wished that when they were in high school their parents had been more proactive about limiting the amount of time they could spend on the computer. Moderation is one thing that most young people are simply not good at. The technology also makes it hard to disengage. After all, a good IM conversation can last all night long, and MySpace is open 24/7! As a result, when kids are able to spend as much time as they want on the computer, they tend to overdo it.

In fact, a number of surveyed high school and college students admitted that their computer use actually cut into the amount of sleep they got and eventually impacted both their health and their grades. Setting appropriate limits on when and how long teens can be on the computer is a healthy way for parents to help young people manage their technology. Most teens are very understanding of the need to limit themselves and are often willing to negotiate with their parents about what those limits should be.

Computer placement. Another guideline recommended by a majority of surveyed parents has to do with where the computer is located. If possible, the computer on which teens talk with their friends should be kept out in the open. While allowing a teen to have a computer in his or her room may be quite tempting, isolation can make some online problems more challenging. After all, it is hard to feel highly intimate with someone when your mom or dad keeps walking by. Talking about sex online or sharing unhealthy pictures may not be quite so tempting when a little brother or sister is sitting in the same room playing video games. Keeping the computer public helps teens keep their computer use on the up and up.

The "no minimization" rule. One rule that works quite well in our house is one that states, "No child may minimize or in any way throw his or her body across the screen to hide something from a perusing parent." This rule works a lot better with my thirteen-year-old who has just begun instant messaging than it does with my eighteen-year-old. He has been using IM a lot longer than I knew it existed, and we have come to an understanding about how much privacy he should have. My thirteen-year-old, however, is just starting out. Together we talked about how we were going to approach the computer, making the deal that, to start with, I could read anything she wrote. As time went on and she demonstrated a fairly mature approach to the computer, I read less and less. Now I ask her if it is okay for me to read something. We still, however, keep the no minimization rule. I can walk by and glance at what she is doing or who she is talking with. It keeps me feeling "in the loop" and keeps her from spending time doing things she shouldn't.

A "netiquette" list. As every parent of teenagers knows, you can't always be with your children, helping them make good decisions. At some point, they start doing that on their own. However, a little push in the right direction never hurts. One exercise that can be particularly helpful, especially with younger teens, is to develop a list of dos and don'ts for talking on the computer. Here are a few that might help get you started:

- **Don't** forward someone's e-mail or IM without his or her permission.
- **Don't** respond to messages from a "cyberbully."
- **Don't** share your password with anyone.

- **Don't** send messages when you are angry.
- **Don't** talk to strangers.
- **Don't** provide personal information.
- **Do** think about what it would feel like to be the receiver of your messages.
- **Do** use only language you would use in person (and only language you would use in front of your parents).
- **Do** take a break after twenty to thirty minutes of computer time.
- **Do** remember that things are not private on the computer.[1]

Technology choices. Kids are so different. Some like computers; others prefer being outside. Some are mature and trustworthy; others are not. Some are ready to use instant messaging and sites such as MySpace; some *definitely* are not. That is where you come in. You need to help your child decide what, if any, technology is best suited for him.

Many parents have found that e-mail is a good place to introduce children into the wide world of communication technology. There are lots of good e-mail programs specifically designed for young users that allow parents to read e-mails before they are delivered, to monitor friends, and even to enforce time limits. E-mail might provide a safe starting space where both you and your child can talk about what it means to be a good online communicator. As your child builds skills and demonstrates trustworthiness, more freedom can easily be offered.

Another starting point might be some of the new social networking sites designed for children who are not yet ready for places like MySpace (see Appendix C). Some sites, such as Club Penguin, are designed for young children and introduce a somewhat monitored approach to online chatting. Other sites, such as Imbee, are for older children but sill require parental approval of friends and offer easy parental monitoring.

Perhaps you and your child decide that IM is the place to start. According to the 2005 Pew Internet and American Life Project, most young people begin instant messaging around twelve or thirteen years of age. While IMing is a bit tamer and more controlled than sites like MySpace, it can still be misused. If your early teenager is easily hurt or has a hard time managing friendships and the related drama, IM may be a bit much. On the other hand, IM does tend to help quiet kids gain confidence and social skills as well as allowing them to stay connected in a way that is convenient and meaningful.

A social networking site like MySpace is a different story. It tends to be used by older teens and requires a certain degree of maturity. While there may be plenty of good things about MySpace, of which your teen will be happy to tell you, MySpace may require much more parent involvement. As one youth pastor constantly reminds me, pornography is always one click away when a kid is on MySpace. That's not to say that every teen will take that click, but you may want to consider your child's ability to show restraint as, together, you decide which technology is most useful—especially for young teens.

A lot of parents are playing catch-up when it comes to their teens' use of online communication technology. If we could have thoughtfully aided our teens in choosing which technology to use, we would have. Instead, we are often simply trying to figure out what they have been up to for the past few years. And if that isn't bad enough, dictating new guidelines after a teen has already incorporated the technology into his or her lifestyle is sort of like fixing the gates after the cows have gotten out. A lot of important work has to be done before those "post-cow-run" gates can be effective—and sometimes those gates just end up getting in the way. If your teenagers are already up to their ears in technology, open discussions about how you can come alongside them to protect and empower them really need to take place before any guidelines are developed.

Step 3: Monitor

Coming up with effective computer-use policies can take a little work. The long-range benefits, however, will make every minute of conversation, compromise, and consequence-setting worth it. Clear, enforceable, and fair guidelines will help teenagers understand their limits and protect kids who are overconfident in their understanding and use of the computer. Once the guidelines are in place, however, is not the time to plop down with a sigh into a big, comfy chair, readying for a long, quiet nap. For next comes the really tricky part—figuring out how best to monitor the children we love, adore, and would love to trust.

Monitoring will look different in every family. Some kids, especially younger teens, need more intensive monitoring. Some, unfortunately, have proven themselves to be untrustworthy. They have gotten in trouble or have misused the computer in a way that was harmful to themselves or someone else. In these cases, parents need to step in and provide the extra motivation the teenagers need to follow the rules and make good choices.

Many kids, however, require much less monitoring. As they get older and demonstrate an ability to use the technology wisely, it makes sense to provide less invasive forms of supervision. After all, the ultimate goal is to end up with well-equipped, thoughtful young adults who are able to navigate the complexities of online communication as they leave the nest and venture into their own new worlds. Following are a number of suggestions parents have made to help monitor the Internet use of their teens, starting with the least intrusive and ending with the most highly involved. It is up to you to decide the healthiest way both to protect and to empower your child.

Instant messaging. When kids were asked what they thought would be the best way for parents to keep track of what their kids were doing online, they consistently suggested that parents keep the lines of communication open. For instance, kids did not like it when their parents read their IM conversations, but they did like it when their parents asked how their friends were doing. Asking things such as "What's new with Jennifer?" or "Who are you talking to?" or "Say hi to Jake for me" were much better received than parents reading entire conversations over their kids' shoulders. These kinds of questions communicate trust in the teenagers and lets them know that their parent is both interested in and informed about important online relationships. In addition to conversation, an occasional slow saunter past an IMer, especially if the "no minimization" rule is in effect, can also remind a teen that he or she is responsible for online actions and that Mom and Dad just may be smarter than they look!

If having your teenager self-report doesn't seem like a strong enough way to keep an eye on what is happening online, you can do some monitoring on your own. Sorting through your children's buddy lists with them will aid you in keeping track of their online contacts. Schedule a regular time to go through the lists and identify which screen names are not being used by friends and which screen names represent people they have not met face-to-face. Some parents also recommend that kids share their passwords with them so the adult can check the teen's buddy list and profile whenever the need arises.

If kids are behaving poorly in their use of instant messaging, technology exists to alert parents to problems. For instance, if kids have been caught doing a lot of swearing online, software packages are available that will send parents e-mail alerts when certain words or phrases are used on instant messaging. This software can also make conversations available to parental control and supervision.

Entire IM conversations can also be recorded. Software such as Dead AIM allows users to save a digital copy of their conversations. IM providers are also making it easier to record conversation. If a child is experiencing difficulty with a friend or being threatened by a bully, this feature can come in very handy. The parent and child can print off a conversation and work together on how to respond. Some parents may feel that they need to read every IM conversation and require their children to save all of their IM sessions. While this may keep kids from experiencing certain online problems, be advised that there are ways for teenagers to circumvent the technology. Be wise as you consider how much instant messaging conversation you will read, and don't depend on the technology to meet all of your monitoring needs.

Social networking sites. In my opinion, a site such as MySpace requires a consistent degree of parental monitoring and supervision. Once you have had a conversation with your teen about MySpace, you should come to an agreement about parental access to his or her profile. While there are plenty of kids who don't need monitoring, my experience is that most parents need to have access to their teens' MySpace or Facebook sites and monitor them regularly. Not only can parents learn a lot about their children, but they can also help keep them accountable. For a real awakening, you may also want to check out the sites of some of your child's friends. If no privacy settings are in place, it seems only fair that you have the same kind of access to teenagers' sites as the general public. These regular inspections will remind teens that what they put on these sites is never private.

As you consider how to monitor MySpace, be aware of a common approach MySpacers take to parental supervision. Many MySpacers report having two separate profiles—one for their friends and one for their parents. When you go online to check your child's profile, don't forget to run a search to see if you can find other sites your child may have created. You may also want to check their friends' sites, since they would probably respond to postings or blogs using their "real" profile rather than their "parent" profile. The key is to be wise and consistent. The best idea of all, however, is to keep communication open.

Possibly the most valuable tip to keep in mind when it comes to teenagers' use of social networking is to monitor your reaction. This advice was shared by a dad whose son had experienced some very difficult things on MySpace. According to this dad, "You can't freak out about the little things, because they will never come to you about the big things." Kids will lie and swear on MySpace. And sometimes they will talk about things that make parents cringe. But try not to overreact. Keeping the lines of communication open is so very important. If your teens feel that they can trust you to listen and understand about things like exaggerations and foul language, they just may feel comfortable talking to you about problems they are having with cybersex, stalking, pornography, bullying, or self-destructive behavior. It is always hard to walk the parenting line between disciplinarian and counselor. I find it is all too easy to fall into the same role I had when my kids were little, scolding them for their every mistake. When the stakes are as high as they are with MySpace, however, we need to try and find a balance that keeps our children behaving appropriately without shutting them out. By engaging them in dialogue about their use of technology, supporting good choices and talking through the bad ones, we can keep things open so that when they do get into trouble, talking to us will be at the top of their list.

Step 4: Find Alternatives

Managing teenagers and their technology can be quite a challenge. At times online communication technology may seem foreign, overwhelming, and just not something we have the skill or energy to tackle. As we seek to understand new technology better, however, let's not forget there are plenty of things that help teens develop their social networks and skills that have nothing to do with computers or cyberspace. Without a doubt, hanging out with friends face-to-face in real life is the best way to get to know one another. One reason kids have become so enamored with online social networking is that in their busy lives, finding time to connect with people who are important to them is difficult. Parents of online teens are therefore challenged to help them find alternative ways to meet their social needs.

For some of us, aiding our teens in developing real-world relationships requires moving our schedules around so we can transport them to places where they can have fun with their friends. Other times it means encouraging them to invite their friends over and providing food and space for some healthy face-to-face time. Sometimes it may require us simply to become more involved in their lives. By finding shared interests or things to work on together, we can intentionally create opportunities for some quality parenting time.

Quite honestly, when I am busy and my kids seem more than happy to sit at their computers, typing away, it is easy to overlook opportunities for interaction. I convince myself that they are doing fine. What I need to do, however, is to be much more intentional about ripping my kids away from their screens and hauling them outside for a game of Frisbee or to the park for a nice walk with the dog. Those are the types of things that will ultimately make me a better parent and my kids more skilled at communicating.

Being the parent of a social-networking, instant-messaging teen feels much more complex than being the parent of a Sesame Street-loving toddler. The stakes seem higher, the kids can be more demanding and deceptive, and the impact can be more far-reaching and complicated. I have days when I dream of how much better life would be without computer technology, and I wish I could just pull the plugs on my children's computers. They have taught me, however, that their technology is valuable to them. It has a part in shaping how they relate to others, how they view themselves, and how they understand their faith. It is time for parents, myself included, to take up the challenge to talk with, train, empower, and pray for (and with) our kids, and ultimately to pull up to the computer to see what the virtual commotion is all about.

YouTube

Entertainment Made to Order

While IM and social networking sites such as MySpace currently dominate the communication technology landscape, there is a new piece of technology speeding over the horizon. According to *TIME* magazine, YouTube has "created a new way for millions of people to entertain, educate, shock, rock, and grok one another on a scale we've never seen before," making enough of a wave to receive *TIME*'s Best Invention of the Year award in 2006.[1]

YouTube is a free, video-sharing website that went online in 2005. It is one of a handful of video-sharing sites that allows users to upload original video content. YouTube, in particular, offers an enormous repository of videos ranging from classic performances by Count Basie and Pablo Casals to clips of Barbra Streisand cursing out hecklers; from presidential hopefuls making racial slurs to guys mixing Diet Coke and Mentos or lonelygirl15 sharing heart-wrenching stories of fictional tragedy. YouTube, and sites like it, provide a new place for kids to go for entertainment. For some, it is a place to display emerging video production skills. For others, it is a way to stay on top of trends in pop culture. For many, it is a way to relax and share a few laughs with friends. Whatever the case, YouTube is most likely the next big thing to hit the world of adolescent technology and communication.

YouTube Users: Who Are They?

According to research done in 2006 and 2007, 42 percent of online adults say they have watched a video on YouTube.[2] Each day about 100 million clips per day are viewed and more than 70,000 new videos are uploaded.[3] YouTube estimates that more than 34 million people access their site each month. While these statistics are fairly convincing, there is no sign that YouTube has reached its peak. It is currently growing at a much faster pace than MySpace and will soon be one of the most used sites on the World Wide Web.

YouTube Uses: What Are They Doing?

There is little doubt that YouTube is big and getting bigger. As technology changes, so will the way kids use it to stay entertained. Therefore, the next logical questions are "How does technology such as YouTube influence how kids think and act?" and "How can we as parents best help our kids use this new technology in ways that are both thoughtful and constructive?" To answer these questions, it's important to get a better feel for how kids use the technology.

Entertainment

Clearly, one of the primary uses of YouTube is entertainment. Kids go to YouTube to get a laugh. Sometimes they will spend hours searching through the site, looking for the perfect video to share with classmates. Other times, they will follow links forwarded by their friends, looking for a good chuckle. You can just imagine how much fun a group of middle school boys can have as they huddle around the computer during a break at school, all watching a video where some kid slams his bike into a wall or sticks marshmallows up his nose. For some middle schoolers, life just doesn't get any better.

Much of the entertainment on these video-sharing sites is manufactured by amateur filmmakers who suddenly feel powerful or noteworthy because they know how to point the camera and say "action." Not surprisingly, most videos would not be considered "high quality" entertainment. I must admit, however, that *some* of the videos are really funny. Many are created by professional or semiprofessional companies and are very well done. Some videos are so creative they take my breath away, while others make me laugh so hard I can't wait to forward them on to unsuspecting friends. YouTube is full of the best and worst our culture has to offer.

Another way YouTube serves as a source of entertainment is in the way it allows teens to get caught up on favorite TV shows they might have missed. According to a number of interviewed students, it just doesn't make sense to try and build a busy schedule around a TV show when they can easily sit and watch the whole thing, whenever they want, just by logging into YouTube. While some of the video clips are put on the Internet by the original producers of the content, many are not. It is no surprise, therefore, that traditional media conglomerates are still trying to determine how best to deal with this huge copyright-infringing, consumer-driven monster. Some networks are establishing their own on-demand sites where viewers can catch up on recent episodes of favorite shows. (For example, Fox owns MySpace, so naturally, you can find that network's prime-time favorites at www.myspace .com/fox.) Deciding to work with the power of YouTube instead of against it, other corporations such as CBS, NBC Universal, and Warner Music group have reached agreements to allow clips of their shows and music videos to be legally uploaded on a regular basis. That means teens can easily watch a Saturday Night Live skit or a music video, whenever they want, free of charge. As a result, the way our kids are consuming traditional media such as television is rapidly changing.

Self-expression

A second role played by YouTube technology has to do with the opportunity it provides young people to express themselves in a medium other than simple text. While blogging has inspired teens to let the world view and interact with their feelings and opinions through writing, vlogging (or video blogging) allows them to express themselves in a way that can communicate with much more creativity and presence. Even though some videos are sweet and meaningful, many more are simple productions uploaded by teens with a little too much time on their hands. It is way for young people to experiment with a visual way of communicating. Whether it be ten mind-numbing minutes of a guy lip syncing to his favorite music or five torturous minutes of girls talking on the phone, the videos highlight how important visual literacy is becoming in our society.

Just as we teach our kids how to read and write, interacting through text, the next generation will need to know how to create and evaluate messages in visual form. YouTube allows young people to use this visual medium to enhance their ability to communicate with one another in a way that is a good fit for today's visually-focused teen. It is quite possible that, in the future, today's Internet text-based social networking will become more centered on visual images, conflating the MySpace and YouTube technologies into one giant, self-expressing, social-networking megasite. For now, however, I have found very few young people who have actually uploaded things to YouTube. At this point in time, it would seem that for many teens, YouTube is more about being entertained than finding a voice for self-expression.

Trendwatching

A third role YouTube plays in the lives of teens is related to trends in pop culture. Once something becomes popular on YouTube, it is only a matter of days before kids and adults around the country are talking about it. For example, take OK Go, a rock band struggling to make the scene. They posted a wonderfully creative video showing band members dancing on treadmills to their latest song "Here It Goes Again." Within the first month, their video was watched more than 3.5 million times. There are very few tools that can so powerfully propel a band from anonymity to stardom in a matter of days. Or take for instance the Saturday Night Live skit titled "Lazy Sunday." It was viewed by millions of YouTubers, and before SNL could yank it from the Net, hundreds of amateur filmmakers made their own spoofs of the skit, many funnier than the original.

YouTube provides a space where pop trends can reach millions at a time. In a way, it unifies culture like very few older technologies have been able to do. Some of these trends are quite positive, restoring one's hope for the future of our high-tech society. For example, police departments from across the country can post crime videos that are viewed by thousands of people. In more than one case, criminals have turned themselves in, knowing their covers had been thoroughly blown. Other positive messages, from the prevention of violence or drugs to presentations of the gospel message, can infiltrate the hearts and minds of teenage pop culture like never before—if the creators of the message are willing to use creativity and humor in a way that hooks into the teenage psyche.

Unfortunately, as much as we'd like to think that technology such as YouTube will enhance positive teenage trends, it can clearly create negative ones as well. Video trends such as those including girl fights, teenage rapes, and just plain stupid youthful behavior can be easily uploaded into the minds of voyeuristic, sensation-seeking young people, often bypassing their moral sense of what is right and wrong. YouTube provides a space where teens can easily participate in a collective culture, being part of both positive and negative trends that shape the way our kids think and behave.

YouTube Challenges: What Are the Problems?

In many ways, in YouTube's emerging technology we are seeing just the beginnings of the next cultural change. Just as the World Wide Web held promises of democracy in action, the little guy taking power away from the big corporations, so, too, does YouTube hold the potential for individuals to have an impact on a large part of our society. Unfortunately, just like other technologies, it also carries with it significant challenges.

The first and most obvious problem with video-sharing sites such as YouTube has to do with the garbage. Just like MySpace, YouTube is *filled* with pornography and violence. The difference is that YouTube allows viewers to experience it all in living color.

At this point, YouTube tries to delete or block pornography to users of all ages and seems to be a bit more successful at doing so than MySpace. As the site grows, however, this challenge will certainly become even more of a problem. Before you sign off on the site and allow your child unmonitored accesses, you need to be aware of the R- and X-rated material that now rests at your child's fingertips as he or she enters the site.

A second challenge with sites like YouTube has to do with some of the warnings sounded by authors such as Neil Postman in *Amusing Ourselves to Death*. He reminds us that

> in an age of advanced technology, spiritual devastation is more likely to come from an enemy with a smiling face than from one whose countenance exudes suspicion and hate. . . . [W]hen a population is distracted by trivia, when cultural life is redefined as a perpetual round of entertainments, when serious public conversation becomes a form of baby-talk, when, in short, people become an audience and their public business is a vaudeville act, then a nation finds itself at risk. . . .[4]

Keep in mind, Neil Postman sounded this warning more than twenty years ago.

Entertainment sites such as YouTube have clearly captured the attention of today's young people. We must, however, ask what it is filling their attention with. According to Anthony Perotta, filmmaker and St. Paul High School teacher, "I think YouTube has made us dumber. . . . We're getting lost in the culture of entertainment where no ideas are being presented."[5] Most YouTube clips are just a few minutes long and few contain any cogent message. One of the long-term drawbacks of technology that allows us to communicate through video clips devoid of any real substance is that our kids are not being challenged to think or act in ethical and thoughtful ways. This, in turn, may make them much less able to deal with temptations that come their way, whether those temptations be materialism and selfishness or violence and pornography. Their ability to critically analyze the destructive messages they receive from their culture may also decrease. And that, my friends, is where we as Christian parents come in.

YouTube Training: Finding the Teaching Moments

One of our jobs as parents is to help our kids learn how to make good decisions and critically analyze the things they see. It may be a bit counterintuitive, but I have found YouTube to be a terrific source of connection with my older son. There have been a number of evenings where he and I sit and together search for good videos. He shows me some of the ones his friends have shared with him, and I find a few I know he will like. In between the videos, we talk about what makes something funny or how the creators could have improved their video. We talk about the kinds of things we each like and what things annoy us. As we search, we talk about the pornography or the violence that pops up and how we can best filter those messages. YouTube times have become pretty special to me, not just because it is a time for me to reconnect with my increasingly independent son, but because, in between the dance clips, the monologues, the cartoons, the video paintings, the flashing Christmas lights, the lip syncing, and the baby laughs, there lie some significant teachable moments.

As parents, we need to be aware of the kind of garbage that is inherent in file-sharing sites such as YouTube. We also need to be willing to share some of the technology with our kids. By sitting with them as they learn to navigate the sites, we can provide the training they need to use it wisely. By sifting through the sites ourselves, we can get a better idea about when our younger children are old enough to begin accessing the sites. As with other technology, it just takes a little intentional parenting on our part. Beginning with conversations about YouTube, finding out what our children think and what they've heard, we can lay the groundwork. From there we can establish workable guidelines about when, where, and how they can use the sites, never forgetting to keep a watchful and monitoring eye out for problems that may pop up. By sharing videos and stories about the site, we can keep in touch with the kinds of things that have captured our children's attention, always being alert for alternative, real-life ways to find a laugh or to tell a creative story. Whether it be MySpace, IM, or YouTube, keep in mind the parenting tips and connection suggestions we discussed earlier in the book: talk, set guidelines, monitor, and find alternatives (see pages 92–101). They provide a workable structure whereby we can help our children manage this emerging technology.

YouTube is an interesting phenomenon that will probably impact our collective culture in ways that few other things have. We want to make sure our kids are able to handle those changes in ways that are thoughtful and based on the values we hope they have learned from us. With a little bit of help, let's pray that it is our kids who are able to rise above the messages they get from their entertainment sources, becoming the agents of change that God has called them to be.

instant message abbreviations

<3 = love
1 = ready
2morow = tomorrow
4NR = foreigner
9 = parent or "other" is in the room
99 = parent or "other" is out of the room
B4 = before
BBL = be back later
bc = because
BF = boyfriend
BFF = best friends forever
BRB = be right back
C/M = call me
CU2M = see you tomorrow
CUL8TR = see you later
GF = girlfriend
GJ = good job
GLHF = good luck have fun
GTG or G2G = got to go
HAGS = have a great summer
IDK = I don't know
JK = just kidding
JP = just playing
KIT = keep in touch
LLOL = literally laughing out loud
LMAS = laughing my a** off

LOL = laugh out loud
LYLAS = love ya like a sister
LYMI = love ya mean it
MYOB = mind your own business
N/M = never mind
NB = newbie
NM = not much
OMG = Oh my gosh
Prec = precious
ROFL = rolling on the floor laughing
RRR = haR, haR, haR (instead of LOL)
Spec = special
T4Y = time for you—time to talk to you
TMI = too much information
TTYL = talk to ya later
TX = thanks
^URS = up yours
W/E = whatever
WTF = what the f***
WTH = what the h***

top 20 instant messaging abbreviations every parent should know

From http://www.netlingo.com/top20teens.cfm

1. POS = parent over shoulder
2. PIR = parent in room
3. P911 = parent alert
4. PAW = parents are watching
5. PAL = parents are listening
6. ASL = age/sex/location
7. MorF = male or female
8. SorG = straight or gay
9. LMIRL = let's meet in real life
10. KPC = keeping parents clueless
11. TDTM = talk dirty to me
12. IWSN = I want sex now
13. NIFOC = nude in front of computer
14. GYPO = get your pants off
15. ADR = address
16. WYCM = will you call me?
17. KFY = kiss for you
18. MOOS = member(s) of opposite sex
19. MOSS = member(s) of same sex
20. NALOPKT = not a lot of people know that

parent resource websites

Parenting Sites

www.mediafamily.org
Lots of good parenting advice—both Internet and media uses

www.safekids.com
Excellent parenting ideas

www.netsmartz.org
Lots of parenting advice from the National Center for Missing & Exploited Children—especially good for elementary-aged kids

www.getnetwise.com
Well-organized parenting and technical advice

www.protectkids.com
Internet safety and parenting site

www.cybersmart.org
Good educator link

http.pta.org
Good articles on a variety of topics, including video games, cell phones, and cyber-love

Filtering Software Information

www.filterreview.com
Helps parents find software to monitor and protect kids on the Internet

www.blogsafety.com
Blog site that lets parents share questions and advice on Internet safety

www.webwisekids.com
Features some parenting tips as well as software for sale

www.contentwatch.com
Distributor of filtering software

Research Site

www.pewinternet.org
Offers the latest research on adolescent use of IM and MySpace

Internet Safety Sites

www.ncmec.org
Website for the National Center for Missing and Exploited Children

www.fbi.gov
The Federal Bureau of Investigation's website has lots of good Internet safety information.

www.isafe.org
Internet safety site

Beginning E-mail for Children

www.zoobuh.com
Zoobuh's software features lots of good parental controls, including monitoring, activity logs, and time monitoring.

www.kidmail.net
An inexpensive way to manage who sends your child e-mails. It has an interactive animated feature for younger children.

www.safe2read.com
For a small monthly fee this software lets you monitor the e-mails your child receives.

Beginning Social Networking

www.clubpenguin.com

A cute site that offers social networking, chat rooms, and games for kids. It uses language filters to make conversations as clean as possible. It does not allow children to post private information.

www.imbee.com

This networking site does a lot of the things that MySpace does but requires that parents approve friends before conversations can take place.

www.nicktropolis.com

A brand-heavy site sponsored by Nickolodeon where kids can chat, play Nick-themed games, watch Nick videos, and hang out in SpongeBob's World.

www.disney.com

Another branded site, at Disney XD, kids watch Disney videos, play Disney-themed games, and customize their own pages.

www.webkinz.com

A branded site for the cute little stuffed animals Webkinz, which can be purchased at many local retailers (from toy stores to Hallmark stores). Your purchase of the stuffed animal provides a code allowing access to the website where children can care for their real/virtual pet, play games, and learn how to operate in a virtual world.

www.whyville.net

Kids can enter this virtual world where nearly 2 million "citizens" help create a virtual economy. They can play games and chat, or visit City Hall and museums. The site is free, but there is third-party advertising.

social networking sites

Most Popular Online Social Networking Sites

www.myspace.com
www.facebook.com
www.xanga.com
www.friendster.com
360.yahoo.com
www.reunion.com

Video Sharing Sites

www.youtube.com
video.google.com
www.broadcaster.com
www.bliptv.com
www.ourmedia.org
www.vsocial.com (combination social networking and video
    sharing)

Christian Social Networking Sites

www.xianz.com
www.holypal.com
www.fellowshipbuilder.com
www.crossfriends.com
www.christianster.com
www.mypraize.com

online glossary

avatar. A digital image that represents an online user. An avatar may be used in an instant messaging program to represent the user, accompanying the person's name on buddy lists and in text boxes. It may be a cartoon figure or any other graphic representation.

chat room. A place where a number of users can interact in real time. Unlike traditional instant message conversations, chat rooms allow everyone in the "room" to see the conversation. Most instant message chat rooms are private, allowing only designated chatters to enter.

download. To transfer computer files from the Internet to an individual computer.

friending. Finding friends on a social network site. Friending happens when a user browses user groups and friends' sites for new friends. Friending is used to achieve the goal of getting as many friends as possible.

gaming. Playing a video or computer game. Many games are played online where users are connected through the Internet. Gamers may play with people they know or, as is often the case, play with users they do not know. Most online games include a chat function similar to that found in instant messaging.

IMvironments. Specialized backgrounds that are used in instant messaging applications. These backgrounds often surround the text box and add color and stylized fonts to the text itself.

minimization. Closing a screen that is currently running on the computer. Minimized screens can easily be opened and closed without affecting the function of the program.

netiquette. Rules of conduct and etiquette used in online communication such as instant messaging and blogging.

shout out. Having a fight online.

text messaging or texting. Sending short text-based messages through mobile devices such as cell phones and PDAs (personal digital assistants).

upload. Transferring a computer file from an individual computer to the Internet.

whore list. List of fictional friends that can be created or purchased to enhance the size of a social networker's friends' list.

endnotes

Chapter 1 Instant Messaging: "Who, Exactly, Is the Messenger, and What Makes Him So Instant?"

1. Wikipedia, s.v., "Instant Messaging," http://en.wikipedia.org/w/index.php?title=Instant_messaging&oldid=53085207 (accessed May 17, 2006).
2. AOL Instant Messenger, http://aim.com/help_faq/starting_out/getstarted.adp?aolp=/ (accessed March 2006).
3. Wikipedia, s.v., "Instant Messaging."
4. Adapted from Angela Gunn, *Ping! The Yahoo! Messenger Guide to All Things IM* (New York: Sterling, 2005).

Chapter 2 Social Networking: "If MySpace Is Their Space, Is Their Space Like My Space?"

1. Figures compiled by Hitwise, cited in G. O'Malley, "MySpace Blossoms into Major Web Portal," *Advertising Age* 77, no. 29 (2006): 4–26.
2. P. Sellers, "MySpace Cowboys," *Fortune* 154, no. 5 (2006): 66–74.
3. Ibid., 69.
4. Figures compiled by the Nielsen/NetRatings, cited in K. Oser, "MySpace: Big Audience, Big Risks," *Advertising Age* 77, no. 8 (2006): 3–25.
5. Ibid.
6. As reported by Hitwise, cited in T. Arnold, "The MySpace

Invaders," *USA Today* (July 31, 2006). http://www.usatoday
.com/tech/hotsites/2006-07-31-myspace-invaders_x.htm.
7. B. Bulik, "How to Make Connection," *Advertising Age* 77, no.
18 (2006): 85.
8. MySpace has a Top 8 while other sites, such as Facebook,
do not.

Chapter 3 The Good: "Why Do My Kids Like the Computer More Than Me?"

1. Pew Internet and American Life Project (2005), http://pewinternet
.org/PPF/r/162/report display.asp (accessed March 2006).
2. Ibid.
3. Ibid.
4. The names and specifics of this example have been changed.

Chapter 4 The Bad: "If It Isn't Real, How Can It Hurt So Badly?"

1. George Barna, *Generation Next* (Ventura, CA: Regal, 1995), 47.
2. Michael Bugeja, *Interpersonal Divide: The Search for Community in a Technological Age* (New York: Oxford University Press, 2005), 3.
3. B. Wellman, A. Quan-Hasse, J. Boase, K. Hampton, et al. "The Social Affordances of the Internet for Networked Individualism," *Journal of Computer Mediated Communication* 8, no. 3 (2003).
4. Quentin Schultz, *Habits of the High-Tech Heart: Living Virtuously in the Information Age* (Grand Rapids: Baker, 2004), 207.
5. John Jewell, *Wired for Ministry: How the Internet, Visual Media, and Other New Technologies Can Serve Your Church* (Grand Rapids: Brazos, 2004), 61.

Chapter 5 Fearless Parenting: "But My Kids Know So Much More Than I Do!"

1. Adapted from M. Braun, *Mom's Survival Guide to Instant Messaging* (Sun Prairie, WI: Sun Prairie Moms, LLC, 2004).

Chapter 6 YouTube: Entertainment Made to Order

1. http://www.time.com/time/2006/techguide/bestinventions/ inventions/youtube2.html.

2. J. Yantosh. "One-third of frequent YouTube users are watching less TV to watch videos online," *PR Newswire US* (January 29, 2007). Research conducted by Harris Interactive.

3. J. Law. "The oddball, online world of YouTube," *Niagara Falls Review* (February 7, 2007), A1.

4. Neil Postman. *Amusing Ourselves to Death* (New York: Penguin Books, 1986), 155.

5. J. Law, A1.